Skin and Blood

SKIN AND BLOOD

A GOSPEL APPROACH TO RACE & RACIAL ANIMOSITY

DOUGLAS WILSON

CANON PRESS

MOSCOW, IDAHO

Published by Canon Press
P.O. Box 8729, Moscow, Idaho 83843
800.488.2034 | www.canonpress.com

Douglas Wilson, *Skin and Blood: A Gospel Approach to Race and Racial Animosity*
©2017, 2022 by Douglas Wilson.

Originally published by Blog & Mablog Press in 2017. Reissued with a new preface by Canon Press in 2022.

Cover design: Jacob Schwander
Interior layout: Valerie Anne Bost

Except where noted, all Scripture quotations are from the King James Version. All Bible quotations marked ESV are from the English Standard Version copyright ©2001 by Crossway Bibles, a division of Good News Publishers. Used by permission.

Library of Congress Cataloging-in-Publication Data forthcoming

22 23 24 25 26 27 28 29 30 31 32   1 2 3 4 5 6 7 8 9 10

Dedicated to Thabiti Anyabwile,
with respect and gratitude.

CONTENTS

CHAPTER 1

WHAT IS RACISM, AND WHY IS IT SINFUL?

I n our modern climate, the more undefined and nebulous a "vile" thing like "racism" is, the better it is for the race-mongers and race-baiters. With lack of definition, they can *always* nail you. Federal bureaucracy got rolling a little slowly after Katrina? Racism. Got your feelings hurt at airport security? Racism. Mark Twain wrote a book a hundred and fifty years ago that had racial epithets in it? Racism. And so on. Of course, racism inflation sets in, and pretty soon the coin is completely debased. When everyone is racist, then nobody is.

Back when the world was more oriented in a right-side-up way than it is now, *racism* was a shorthand way of describing the mental outlook of the bigot—and everybody knew what a bigot was, also. *Racism* was a descriptive term, and I did not mind describing racism as a sin against God, which I have done for many decades now. And if we are using normal, old-school definitions, racism really is a sin against God.

But we have gotten to the point where the word is not only useless, but is also pernicious. It has now come to be applied willy-nilly to virtually everything in the Western world, from microaggressions to expressing the view at Tea Party rallies that budgets should balance. Racism is, as a wit once explained, winning an argument with a liberal. It has become pernicious because if racism is a sin, then prejudice is, also, and if prejudice is a sin, then discrimination is, also. And the racism and the prejudice and the discrimination float over the perpetrator's head like an inchoate cloud of undefined but still untoward thoughts. And this is how we have gotten to the point where a person is thought to be messed up if he discriminates about anything. So I would be quite happy in principle to throw the word overboard as being now worthless, and refuse to use it anymore. But when we had done so, we would immediately need *another* word to describe those folks who really are ... racist. And so, in the meantime, we need a working definition.

I hope it is clear that the word *racist* should not be routinely or automatically applied to the following: someone to my political right, someone who thinks that anyone named Muhammad should receive extra scrutiny at airports, a medical researcher who believes that one race may be vulnerable to a disease that the others are not, and so on. There are many positions that are related to race that may even in fact be wrong, and yet should not be labeled racist. Nor should we label someone as a racist simply for believing that the races are different. Of course they are different. If they were not different, we wouldn't be having this discussion because no one could tell what we were talking about.

In my book *Black and Tan*[1], I quote the philosopher David Stove who makes a very similar point when arguing against the phrase *racial prejudice*. When we make *prejudice* the problem (pre-judging), then the solution is clearly to be found in education. Ignorance is the problem; education for the humanist is always the savior. He argued that we should use the phrase *racial animosity* instead. Animosity is not something that can be fixed by education—it is an old-fashioned *sin*.

But the Bible doesn't ever describe racism as a sin. Rather, I believe the Bible identifies two sins in particular that always arise in the sinful heart whenever we have interaction between cultures, races, castes, sexes, fifth and third graders, nations, or two Texas football rivals that shall remain unnamed lest violence break out. Those two sins are malice (or animosity) and vainglory respectively. Malice is hatred that is not grounded in the Scriptures. There is of course obedient hatred (which we would never think to call malicious). In this sense, it is all right to hate child abuse, genocide, and the way fundamentalist Muslims treat women. But it is not all right to hate someone simply because he is from South Dakota (or Saudi Arabia), or because his mother is French, or because his skin is darker than yours. In other words, when hatred and malice are thrown out at the world on arbitrary and autonomous grounds not found in Scripture, then the real problem is

---

1. *Black and Tan: Essays and Excursions on Slavery, Culture War, and Scripture in America* (Moscow, ID: Canon Press, 2005).

the hatred, not the bogus reasons for it. Now people bond to the strangest things, and sometimes they bond to different kinds of antipathies. One man hates the Jews, another the blacks, another the French, and so on. The problem is the hatred—the despised race is simply the raw material they need to have in order to sin this way. They must have an enemy, they must have a cause. An edifying book to read in this regard is *The True Believer* by Eric Hoffer.[2] Some of his applications are screwy, but his central point is dead on. There are people who need to have an enemy, and racial markers provide them with a handy-dandy uniform for the other side that won't wash off.

Vainglory is simply a form of pride, and pride is the root and mother of all sins. It may not be malicious, but it is still sinful—supercilious, patronizing, boastful, and so on. But what do you have, St. Paul says, that you did not receive as a gift? And if as a gift, then why do you boast as though you did not? Let him who boasts, Paul says, boast in the Lord (1 Cor. 4:7; 1:31).

So I would urge Christians to stop using the phrase "racism is sin," and instead start saying that "racial vainglory is sin" or "racial animosity is sin." But as long as we do continue to use the word *racism*, here is my working definition: A *malicious racist* is someone who directs malice, spite, or hatred toward another human being of another race *because* that person belongs to that other race. A *patronizing racist* is someone who takes personal ego credit for any superiority he may have (whether real or imagined, usually imagined) over someone who belongs to another

---

2. Eric Hoffer, *The True Believer: Thoughts on the Nature of Mass Movements* (New York: Harper & Row, 1951).

race. Often arguments for innate genetic superiority of one race over another are not the racism itself, but are a nearly universal way of buttressing that kind of racism. But the issue is always the "personal ego credit."

A racist, then, is someone who takes the scripturally insufficient grounds of racial differences to justify his own malice or petty pride. And those who do such things need to repent. I cannot imagine any basic arguments of certain whites against blacks (moral, cultural, historical, etc.) that could not have been advanced (with equal justification and force) by first-century Jews with regard to Gentiles. But Scripture rejects all such carnal "wisdom." And despite this great and very real barrier between Jew and Gentile, the bulk of the New Testament is *about* their reconciliation. In this sense, racial, ethnic, and tribal reconciliation is one of the central aspects of the gospel.

When it is stated this way, it is evident that the problem is a moral one, and that the solution is repentance and forgiveness. Only Jesus can remove vainglory and hatred.

STRUNK AND WHITE SUPREMACY

You will not be at all surprised to learn that the biblical definitions I espoused above have not yet been heartily embraced by all the world. The battle over editorial control of the dictionary rages on. That battle, as I have been noting for some years now, is the nature of this cultural conflagration that we are all going through . . . while some in the back are still stoutly maintaining "this is fine." What with all the pronoun nonsense now showing up in the liver, lungs, and brain, this thing appears to have metastasized into our books of grammar. We are badly diseased with regard to vocabulary, grammar, and syntax, and what we desperately need is for someone to write an elegant little volume of sane English usage that will make us all whole again. We need a little *Strunk and White Supremacy*.

Change the metaphor. We have a problem, and the problem is one of hyperinflation. If accusations of racism came in a currency like the *Papiermark*, and they do, what it amounts to is that we have so much of it sitting around in piles now that it is worth nothing anymore. The printing presses are hot, and you can't even buy a paper clip with paper currency anymore. Being a racist today is like becoming a millionaire in the Weimar Republic.

What we need is a return to the gold standard of Scripture. Scripture, and only Scripture, defines sin. That includes any sin having to do with ethnicity. Which means, again, that ethnic vainglory is sinful and to be despised, that ethnic animosity is sinful and to be despised, and that what the world is currently calling the sin of "racism" is not a sin at all. It was a dubious currency when they first started using it, but now their racism is worthless in the description of any sinful attitude. You couldn't buy a used popsicle stick with any amount of it.

TWO SHOOTINGS, DAYS APART

On March 16, 2021, a 21-year-old man went on a shooting spree in Atlanta. Most of the victims were Asian, and the perpetrator was white. Then, on March 22, came a shooting in Boulder, Colorado, where the alleged shooter was a Muslim named Ahmad Al-Issa, and the victims were all white. According to the received totalitolerance wisdom, if you failed to note the racial component in the former situation, you are a racist, and if you took any note of the racial component in the latter situation, you are also a racist.

The real issue here is that if you don't see the politiscam that is being run on you, you are what Bugs Bunny would call a maroon.

RACISM AIN'T WHAT IT USED TO BE

So let me confront the elephant in the room. Some of you may have heard from various unreliable sources that I am a racist. I have written books like *Black and Tan* and have described myself before as a paleo-confederate and other such monstrosities. And confronted with such undeniable facts as these, I remain singularly unapologetic. This causes some people to imitate the hot froth on top of your average Starbucks drink, and the word *indignant* doesn't really begin to cover it.

Because these baseless lies have been widely circulated, I actually have a link on the front page of my blog that reporters can click on if they want to find out what I believe about the human race and ethnic sin. Here it is for you:

God created the entire human race in our first parents, and He did so intending a glorious and variegated unity. "And hath made of one blood all nations of men for to dwell on all the face of the earth, and hath determined the times before appointed, and the bounds of their habitation" (Acts 17:26). When our first parents disobeyed Him by eating the forbidden fruit, they plunged that entire human race into spiritual darkness. This meant that we began to sin by means of everything we could lay our hands on — whether it was sex, metallurgy, tribalism, architecture, or music. If we interacted with it at all, we began to sin with it. After the judgment at Babel scattered us into all different directions, this became profoundly true of our ethnic groupings, and so our tribal enmities both grew and hardened over generations.[3]

I continue on, unrepentant.

With the coming of Christ, God signaled that His purposes in redemption would touch even this, and so the gift of the Spirit at Pentecost indicated that the curse of Babel was now to be reversed in Christ. In Him, we "have put on the new man, which is renewed in knowledge after the image of him that created him: where there is neither Greek nor Jew, circumcision nor uncircumcision, barbarian, Scythian, bond nor free: but Christ is all, and in all." (Col. 3:10–11).

And then, still unrepentant, I go on to identify, as I have already done in this chapter, those things related to ethnicity that Scripture would regard as sinful.

So as we labor to eradicate ethnic sin from our lives, there are two basic forms that ethnic sin can take in the Scriptures. One is when a person's membership in a particular tribe is used as a foundation for justifying malice or enmity toward members of a different group. The second is when it is used as a foundation for a false pride or sense of inflated superiority. The two sins are therefore

3. This and the following two quotes are from Douglas Wilson, "Critical Questions," *Blog & Mablog*, https://dougwils.com/critical-questions.

ethnic enmity and ethnic vainglory, and they are both hated by a holy God. But they are not more radically evil than any other forms of enmity or vainglory, grounded on other baseless trumperies. The sin is always the same kind of blind folly, and Christ died for all of it.

Now, if this is racism, then racism ain't what it used to be, and perhaps you all ought to consider becoming racists also.

But this clear vindication may well leave some of you muttering discontentedly because you feel, somehow, some way, I have brought these charges of racism down on my own head, and that I should try to explain *that*.

I will tell you what I think it is, in all honesty. My offense is that I saw the beast slouching toward Bethlehem a few decades before others did. That is my crime. The onset of our current cultural frenzy did not begin when the Beatles came to America. It began with Rousseau, and the French Revolution, and those seeds of secular totalitarianism. There was a clear direction to all of it that can be traced through nineteenth-century America, and our War Between the States was no small part of it.

And because, in the modern parlance, a racist is anyone who is winning arguments with leftists, and I have been *that* kind of a racist for some decades now, ongoing and very strident attempts have been made to sideline me. The good news is that it is not working. I say this to the current race hustlers—*your* racism is a sham and a cheat.

GO HOME, AMERICA

So I am not here as a white man standing my ground. I *happen* to be white, and that by itself is worth precisely nothing before the throne of Christ. This next point is not made from a position of situated ethnicity. It is not a sampling of white supremacy. It is not an example of someone spouting off while sitting on the cushions of white privilege.

No. What I am is a Christian standing my ground. What I am is a Christian minister who is refusing to cooperate with all the regnant nonsense. Somebody needs to tell America what to do, and here it is. "Go home, you're drunk."

The problem is not that whites hate blacks or that blacks hate Jews or that any given sinner hates any other given sinner. Those things are the fruit of the central problem, but the central problem is that America hates Christ. And because we hate Christ, and the name of Christ, we are hating the only one who can deliver us from our current insanity. Hating Christ is just another phrase for "hating salvation," or "hating deliverance."

But if America does go home, and does sleep it off, then I would invite our poor bedraggled sinner of a nation to come back to church. No more need to tell our country to go home. Rather, the invitation now is to *come* home. Come to Christ. Repent and believe. Chuck all the nonsense. Stop blustering. Stop slandering the preachers who tell you the truth.

Christ died, and was buried, and rose again from the dead. Because of that, and only because of that, America can be delivered. There is no other way. No other name.

Come home.

CHAPTER 2

THE ONLY COLOR
THAT MATTERS

Outside of Jesus Christ, racial harmony is a pipe dream. Apart from Christ, racial reconciliation is not going to happen, but rather the opposite. In Christ, racial harmony is a theological necessity, a doctrinal requirement, and an eschatological hope.

Not only is the secular dream of "one humanity" far beyond the secularists' grasp, it is also beyond the grasp of weak sister evangelicals who for some mysterious reason have adopted the secularist vision of racial harmony instead of the Christian one. This, despite the fact that the impotence of the secularist form of it grows more apparent by the minute, and despite the fact that the Scriptures are so plain on the basis for our reconciliation in Christ.

White and black cannot get along because their blood is red in common, but they *can* get along because Christ's blood was red and uncommon, and was shed for the express purpose of making one new man out of the two, and, in addition, of making one new man out of the seventy. God is building a new humanity in Christ, and there is no new humanity outside of Him.

> And they sung a new song, saying, Thou art worthy to take the book, and to open the seals thereof: for thou wast slain, and hast redeemed us to God by thy blood out of every kindred, and tongue, and people, and nation .... (Rev. 5:9)

> Where there is neither Greek nor Jew, circumcision nor uncircumcision, Barbarian, Scythian, bond nor free: but Christ is all, and in all. (Col. 3:11)

> There is neither Jew nor Greek, there is neither bond nor free, there is neither male nor female: for ye are all one in Christ Jesus. (Gal. 3:28)

We serve and worship a cosmopolitan Christ, and there is no cosmopolis apart from Him.

But in order to come to Him, we must repent and believe. Repent of what? We must repent of the sinful things we were doing. Whites must repent of white sins, and blacks must repent of black sins. You can repent the other guy's problems all day long, and at the end of the day there is no forgiveness for *you*.

I am writing as a minister of Christ, so on one level my color is irrelevant. My commission to speak was not color coded. But it also happens that I am a white man, so let us begin with white sins.

Let us begin with the slave trade, which was obviously no bagatelle. The iniquitous Middle Passage was the death of at least two million kidnapped Africans and the ungodly enslavement of millions of others. The image of God in these slaves was rebelliously denied and arrogantly insulted by an ostensibly Christian civilization. The South was willing to receive a particular kind of human soul as chattel, contrary to the Scriptures they appealed to, and the North, in high hypocrisy, was willing to get rich off a trade that it simultaneously pretended to despise. In the aftermath of Reconstruction, a host of restrictive laws and customs enforced by bigots helped solidify and institutionalize the love-hate relationship of whites and blacks in America. Anybody who thinks it is all hate doesn't get out much, and anybody who thinks it is all love lives under a rock.

With the rise of progressivism, Margaret Sanger founded Planned Parenthood as a way of dealing with all these black "human weeds" and co-opted numerous race quislings to help her encourage black people to line up quietly and cooperate with this eugenics sanitation crew. The end result is that *down to the present day*, a hugely disproportionate number of black children—let us call them "unarmed citizens"—are chopped up into bits in America's abortion mills. These abortion mills were authorized by a predominantly *white* Supreme Court and have been regularly funded by an overwhelmingly *white* Congress. From the time the *Roe v. Wade* decision was handed down until, by the great kindness and mercy of God, it was reversed by *Dobbs v. Jackson*, over 63 million American children were executed. Thirty-five percent of them have been black children. And many of them have had their bodies taken off to market and *sold for parts*. The market in black flesh has not died. Nothing has changed except the scale, which has gone up. In Africa, blacks sold blacks to whites, who knew how to make a profit off that kind of thing. We are doing the same thing now—blacks selling blacks to whites, who compensate for their massive guilt by making sure to buy fair trade coffee.

And then, if a black child successfully runs this gauntlet and makes it into America alive, a bunch of insufferable white people have conspired to subsidize a system whereby young black mothers are given strong financial incentives to not marry the father of their baby. And so we have gotten what we have paid for, which is a pandemic of fatherlessness in the black community. That pandemic is the bottom layer of our cycle of crime and lawless behavior.

So then, black sins. I am just going to mention three. When you have been terribly wronged, as blacks certainly have been, the temptation—and it is a pressing one—is to give way to bitterness.[1] But God's solution to these things is forgiveness, not settling scores. Bitterness offers no salvation whatever. And outside of Christ, there is no such thing as forgiveness. The problem with settling scores is that they never ever get settled. We have more than a few ethnic groups in the world still fighting over things that started many centuries ago. This goes back to the point I made at first, which is that Christ's forgiveness is the only gospel that can enable anybody in this sorry world to

1. Visit http://freefrombitterness.squarespace.com for Jim Wilson's teaching on the topic of bitterness.

start over. There is no other regeneration. Grace can get at things that law cannot.

Second, in the grip of a bitterness that tries to project, it is easy to forget everybody has to operate in their own micro-corner of this great macro-story, and that, however objectionable the large narrative is, not every instance at street level is an instance of the same thing. What hard evidence is there that the attempted arrest of Eric Garner was racially motivated? Give me more than that it can be made to fit in a racialist narrative. In the real world, the actual narrative has many gaps. But an all-encompassing bitterness tries to fill in those gaps, frequently unhelpfully.

Let me give you a thought experiment. For some reason you are in a strange city, and you have to use the subway to get back to your residence, and it is late at night. You go down to the subway platform, which is completely deserted with the exception of three young black men in hoodies, leaning against the wall. They could be waiting for the subway, just like you, or maybe not. Note that I have not in any way indicated the race of the "you" in this thought experiment. Now if you quicken your pace, even if just mentally, or if you in any way brace yourself, if you make a mental note of possible escape routes—is all this coming from the wickedness of a prejudicial heart?

I don't think so. Every human brain has a department of risk assessment, and the guys down in that department are running their calculations all the time. It is a simple fact that black males are disproportionately incarcerated for violent crime. Is this because discrimination disproportionately targets them? Or because they are disproportionately more likely to be guilty of such crime? Or a combination? Whatever you personally believe the answer to those questions might be, you are still down in the subway at one a.m., and you still have to decide what to do.

Third, in addition to bitterness and resentment, there is another temptation to give way to opportunism. Too many blacks allow race-hustlers like Al Sharpton and Jesse Jackson to speak for them and in their name. Those men are not pursuing justice, but rather the main chance. And whenever someone like Voddie Baucham speaks the truth about it, *he* is the one who gets assaulted as a race traitor, with all the real collaborators left alone.

This opportunism is willing to have things *given* when what blacks really needed was to be given a true and honest opportunity to *earn* them. Affirmative action represents the triumph of the soft bigotry of low expectations, which has resulted in a cloud of suspicion cast over every genuine black accomplishment. Affirmative action—another grievous white sin, just us being our patronizing selves.

The end result of that blindness is that we had President Obama wafted to the highest office in the land on the gusts of a group hug approach to racial reconciliation. Once he got there, two things became immediately apparent. One was his lack of any real competence and the other was his ideological commitment to the agenda of the Left, up to and including the abortion industry's contempt for black lives. So *anybody* who voted for Obama—whose legal vision on abortion is simply a more sanitary version of Kermit Gosnell's—has absolutely no right to the phrase "black lives matter." If you voted for Obama, then shut up, leave the protest, and go home. Throw your "black lives matter" sign in the nearest dumpster, and try to retrieve your conscience from that dumpster. If you think that partial birth abortion, performed on a black child, *ought to be fully legal constitutional act*, then you need to come to grips with the fact that the race problem in America is not ultimately cops in NYC—the race problem in America is *you*. And if you are a white evangelical working on racial reconciliation, and you voted for Obama, especially the second time, then all this goes double.

When the apostle Paul was once guilty of an ethnically insensitive slur, he said, quoting a Cretan prophet, that Cretans were evil beasts, lazy gluttons, and liars. This testimony, he said, was true. "Therefore," he said, "rebuke them sharply, that they may be sound in the faith" (Titus 1:13).

So anyone who believes that any racial group cannot be sound in the faith—that's a racist. And anyone who believes that any racial group gets a free pass and does not have to respond to the authoritative Word of the Lord Jesus Christ—calling every color of sinner to repent and believe—that's a racist too.

I do not say any of this as a race pundit, but rather as a race prophet. Thus saith the Lord ...

Thus saith the Lord. It is true that whites don't understand the problems and temptations that blacks confront. It is equally true that blacks don't understand the problems and temptations that whites face. The only one who perfectly understands our tangled lives down here is our great high priest. This high priest, who actually does understand "what it is like," is our *Lord*, and He has told us how to live. *The only one who understands has told us what to do*. We are to repent our sins, believe in Him, follow Him, and love one another. If we don't want to do any part of this, we do not get to say that it is because "He doesn't understand." Because He does.

And His cross deals with real sins, not imaginary ones. It deals with real sins by offering free and full forgiveness. It "deals" with imaginary sins by enabling us to see them for what they are—vain constructions of our own imaginations.

When it comes to issues of race, the cross of Christ puts to death all enmity, hatred, spite, bitterness, and envy. "Having abolished in his flesh the enmity, even the law of commandments contained in ordinances; for to make in himself of twain one new man, so making peace; And that he might reconcile both unto God in one body by the cross, having slain the enmity thereby" (Eph. 2:15–16). In the cross, God crucified racial enmity. He killed hostility, and because Jesus really died, He killed it dead—but only in Christ.

Because liberals believe that man is basically good, they have identified the culprit as "prejudice," or "discrimination." In this scenario, everybody is supposed to mean well, but must be instructed on the proper ways of staying out of microaggressions. This can work for a time. If you hector people enough about the little things, they will stuff the big things. For a time.

But then something happens, or a series of things happen, and all the pent-up animosity erupts. Now the thing to remember about an animosity eruption is that by this time in the cycle nobody cares what you think of them. You try to remonstrate with them . . . "But that's racist!" And they reply, "So?"

In recent years we've seen both anti-cop protesters chanting, "What do we want? Dead cops! When do we want it? Now!" and pro-cop demonstrators wearing "I Can Breathe" T-shirts in a wildly tone-deaf misappropriation of Eric Garner's last words. If you point out how inflammatory this is, both ways, you will be surprised to discover that being inflammatory was the point.

Liberal bromides cannot deal with this. Feel-good gospel coalitiony group hugs can't deal with it. Those with an impotent message have to pretend that racial animosity is really a matter of petty bigotry, because they think they have a message that can handle petty bigotry. But in order to deal with racial animosity, racial hatred, racial hostility, Jesus had to die and rise. The good news is that He did so.

Because He rose from the dead, black men can repent of their envy, hatred, and resentment. Because He died as a perfect sacrifice for sin, white men can repent of their insolence and contempt. And we have gotten to the point in this story of ours, where this message—the death of race hate in the death of Jesus—is a message that needs to be preached. Because of the nature of the message, the color of the one preaching it is irrelevant. The only color that matters is how red the blood was.

The unity our nation needs—and we *do* desperately need it—is not a "group hug" unity, and it is not that kind of unity with a Jesus shine put on it. The message is not "Jesus could help us to like each other better," although that *would* be a downstream consequence. The message we rather need to hear, and which the church needs to declare, is "Jesus forgives our sins."

Before we can have unity in Christ the risen, we must have unity in Christ the crucified. *But this means unity in sin.* This is not going to happen unless we repent of our *own* sins. We need to repent of our white sins and repent of our black sins. To whatever extent you identify with any group, you must identify also with the sins of that group. This is not to the exclusion of identifying with their virtues or strengths, their culture or heritage. It is simply a shared *gospel* identification, and not a *carnal* identification.

We must find common ground in Adam. We must find common ground in our shared iniquity. That is the only way out. When we recognize that we are all one great mess in Adam, then we can by the grace of God shake hands in the second Adam — and only there.

The only true victim in all of this is Jesus Christ, and every color of fist drove the nails in. Let me be specific. What did Jesus die for? "For we ourselves were once foolish, disobedient, led astray, slaves to various passions and pleasures, passing our days in malice and envy, *hated by others and hating one another*" (Titus 3:3, ESV).

I am marking that last phrase — "hated by others, and hating one another." That is what we are doing, right this minute. When sinners fight with other sinners, the problem is never one of finding a plausible target. The problem with the spirit of accusation is that it is diabolical and destructive, not that it is inaccurate. The flaming darts of the evil one frequently find a suitable target. But there is a difference between the condemnation offered by the devil and the spirit of conviction offered by the Spirit of God. They both strike at the darling sin, but one with a cudgel and the other with a surgeon's scalpel.

As we've seen from the lists above, when it comes to race relations in America, absolutely *no one* has a right to a high horse.

So back to black and white. To compare ourselves to the "other group" as though abominations were graded on a curve is like guards at Buchenwald sneering at the guards at Auschwitz for their manifest moral inferiority. Was not their slaughter count *much* higher?

The only thing we should do with our sins is mourn for them, repent of them. We do not get to compare them to the sins of the "others" as a means of justifying ourselves. The only justification of ourselves that any of us could possibly receive is the free grace that is offered through Jesus Christ—free grace to the undeserving. Blacks and whites have a shared legacy in Adam. But it is not a unity to be proud of. It just demonstrates a shared need for the Savior of all mankind.

In short, there will never be unity in the crown without unity in the cross. We all need it, and no one needs it "less" than that other despised group does.

CHAPTER 3

THE HARD BIGOTRY OF LOW EXPECTATIONS

I n the last chapter, I used the phrase "soft bigotry of low expectations," which was coined by George W. Bush (or his speechwriter) and is laden with worldview wisdom. When someone is growing up in a world in which he is confronted with all sorts of unfair challenges, there is a natural and sentimental reaction that wants to soften the challenges instead of hardening the challenger.

The end result is that we wind up placing yet *another* challenge in front of the poor kid. We lower the standard in order to make it easier for him, which actually just puts an asterisk next to all his future accomplishments, if there are any. The asterisk says, "This accomplishment may or may not be the result of this individual's talent or industry."

TWO STORIES

Allow me to begin with the juxtaposition of two incidents.

Quite a few years ago, in the early days of Logos School, I was teaching a class. I remember that it was upper elementary or junior high, somewhere in that neighborhood. I also remember that there was a young black student in the class, and he was not really a great student and was something of a pill. And I recall a parent-teacher conference I had one time with his mom, in which she appeared insufficiently aware of how much of a pill he was being. He was not popular with the other kids, and she, naturally enough, attributed this to their problems with his race. We also discussed his school work. But rather than argue with his mother about whether or not he was being a pill regarding the other kids and a slacker regarding his work, I took a different tack.

I granted her point that he was growing up in a bigoted world, one in which he would have to work twice as hard as the privileged kids in order to achieve the same results. I granted her that, but then said that, as his teacher, I needed to inform her that he was currently working *half* as hard. Given the nature of the world he was growing up in, what do you think is going to happen to him? That's one story.

Then comes Kate Brown, governor of the People's Republic of Oregonistan, who in 2021 signed a measure that removed reading, writing, and math requirements for graduation from Oregon schools, and she did this foul deed in order to *help* students of color.

You see, in the world of unbearable whiteness that Kate Brown inhabits, teaching black kids to do math is a bridge too far. For normal people, hearing this, what word comes to mind? *Insufferable. Patronizing. Exasperating.*

Dreadful. Arrogant. Troublesome. Rebarbative. Grotesque. Insolent. Actually, lots of words come to mind. Here's another one: *Racist.*

Yes, I know. *Racist* has been done to death. Everything is racist, which means that nothing is. Math is racist, and so we'd better not inflict any of that Jim Crow geometry on the hapless black kids. Parallel lines never meet, which reminded somebody of separate drinking fountains, and they were offended by it. Two lines, separate but equal, *ha!*

So we do live in times of racism inflation, and that really must be acknowledged. We are on our guard when it comes to calling each and every little thing racist. The race hustlers, and the soft evangelicals who love to enable them, have inflated the paper currency of racism, such that accusations of racism now have almost no purchasing power—lying there like so many Weimar Papiermarks in the gutter. If somebody yells *racist!* now the best thing to do is to yawn and walk on by. But every once in a while, once in a blue moon, we can still come across the real thing, not inflated paper but an actual gold nugget, and not some worthless paper racism. Every once in a while a gold nugget gets elected to the governor's office in Oregon.

"You are black, or Hispanic, or a Pacific Islander, and so we are going to help you out by not requiring you to learn any basic life skills. Glad we could be of assistance."

And it is all done with a beaming smile, the kind of patronizing smile that absolutely sums up the subtitle of Thomas Sowell's great book *The Vision of the Anointed.* That subtitle is "Self-congratulation as a Basis for Social Policy."

More on all of that shortly.

GEORGE ORWELL, CALL YOUR OFFICE. NO, REALLY, CALL YOUR OFFICE

It may seem to you that I am changing the subject, but I am doing nothing of the kind. Absolutely all of this foolishness is connected.

In 2021, George Orwell's estate approved the publication of a feminist retelling of Orwell's great novel *1984*. Because that is what the world needs right now—to have Orwell's estate approve in principle the idea of "every book rewritten"—and as we have embarked on this brave new publishing world, why not provide an edifying example to start with by rewriting *1984*?

But let us learn wisdom from Orwell, Alice, and Isaiah.

Every record has been destroyed or falsified, every book rewritten, every picture has been repainted, every statue and street building has been renamed, every date has been altered. And the process is continuing day by day and minute by minute. History has stopped. Nothing exists except an endless present in which the Party is always right.[1]

"When I use a word," Humpty Dumpty said in rather a scornful tone, "it means just what I choose it to mean—neither more nor less."

"The question is," said Alice, "whether you can make words mean so many different things."[2]

Woe unto them that call evil good, and good evil; That put darkness for light, and light for darkness; That put bitter for sweet, and sweet for bitter! (Isaiah 5:20)

1. George Orwell, *1984* (London: Secker & Warburg, 1949), chapter 5.
2. Lewis Carroll, *Through the Looking Glass* (London: Macmillan, 1872), 124.

The key to understanding our debates in the public square in these demented times is the simple fact that we are inhabiting an "endless present in which the self-congratulation is always right." They are right by definition, for they are the Anointed, and they can oscillate between whatever positions they want, and those who are opposed to them are the racists, whatever the policy in question may be. That is how the memory hole works.

Did you turn *down* a black kid at the adoption agency? You are a racist. Did you *adopt* a black kid at the adoption agency? You are a colonizing racist. To reapply Chesterton, it is starting to look as though white people are not heinous enough to commit any crime, but rather that any stick is good enough to beat white people with.

SELF-CONGRATULATION AS SUPERPOWER

Let us return to our earlier juxtaposed stories.

According to our modern dictionary despots, the guy (me) who wanted a young black student to learn to stand on his own feet, earn his own way, and to become a valuable, contributing citizen *who had no asterisk by his name* is a racist. I would be tarred as a racist because, my enemies would say, I clearly implied in that story that blacks were lazy. No, my retort would be, I did not say that blacks were lazy. I said that it was *possible* for blacks to be lazy, just as this one was being, and I wanted to work hard at correcting the problem.

And the governor of Oregon, who took all the nets and balls away so that black athletes might start earning their fair share of tennis trophies, is mysteriously a champion of black athletic achievement. The nets and balls were getting in the way of the current goal.

No matter how absurd the claim might be, those who are in the grip of this self-congratulatory fever can overcome, they think, any obstacle. They can defeat any foe, by the simple expedient of definition. That person over there opposes our efforts at self-congratulation, and is therefore by definition a racist, misogynistic colonizing homophobe. By definition.

This claim is made by them because they are actually aspiring to deity, and one of the prerogatives of deity is creating things out of nothing. "And god said, 'let there be racism,' and there was racism. And the evening and the morning were the first hate crime." When our God created the world, He immediately said that it was very good. But when these tin-plated idols create their world filled with various arbitrary sins *ex nihilo*, they shake their heads and say that it is all very, very bad. Or they would shake their heads if only their necks could move.

Of course the downside to all of this is that it is irrational madness. It is what Van Til called integration downward into the void. It is frenzy and confusion. It is the root of all damnation.

Those who call for Nonsense will find that it comes.[3]

MERE GOSPEL, MORE GOSPEL

We are in the trouble we are in because we have walked away from the gospel. And when you walk away from

---

3. C.S. Lewis, *That Hideous Strength* (New York: Macmillan, 1965), 372.

the gospel, you walk away from what only the gospel can provide. Let Thomas Brooks speak to you from across a few centuries:

> What goes from a people when the gospel goes? Answer: peace, prosperity, safety, civil liberty, true glory, and soul-happiness, the presence of God.[4]

What on that list have you not seen evaporating in the last several years? And the reason this is happening is straightforward and plain. We have rejected God, and God is bringing His judgments down upon us.

Our situation is bewildering, but only from inside the rebellion. Sin is confusion. Sin frustrates and lies. Sin is darkness. Sin is lawlessness, and sin steps out into the void. Sin seeks out the abyss, and feels the pull and the draw of that vacuum. Sin is destructive and malicious, and on the way to Hell itself just wants to see the rest of the world burn. Sin wants to scratch and maul. Sin is a devouring beast, but in the end it devours only itself.

If you step outside the rebellion and look at it from that vantage, the whole thing becomes plain. The difficulty is that you cannot step outside the sin of autonomy in any autonomous way. You can't, on your own, go check on what I am saying. The only way to get a true perspective on the madness that is afflicting us is by abandoning the sin of irrational autonomy, which is repentance, and by calling on Christ, which is faith. And there it is, as plain as day, the way out. Repent and believe.

4. C.H. Spurgeon, ed., *Smooth Stones Taken from Ancient Brooks* (New York: Sheldon & Company, 1860), vi.

There is no salvation for our nation without a Savior, and there is no Savior other than Christ. Christ is the only way out. There are those, afflicted by this peculiar frenzy of ours, who want to call this simple presentation of the simple gospel a disparaging name, like "Christian nationalism." What? If I am preaching at an inner city soup kitchen, is that Christian winoism? If I am presenting the gospel to a wicked nation, calling them to repent, that is somehow setting up that sinful nation as an idol? Okay, suit yourself. Jonah's problem was that he was making an idol out of Nineveh?

Do you want reparations? Then look to the cross. That is the only place you will find reparations. Do you want justice? Then look to the cross. That particular injustice was the place where God's holy justice was fully satisfied. Do you want God to deal with white sins, black sins, male sins, female sins, rich sins, poor sins? If you only want Him to deal with *half* of that list, then you are still in your sins. You cannot receive what you are unwilling for God to give to someone else also. Even though you are descended from slaves, if you are unwilling for the sons of slave owners to be forgiven, then you cannot be forgiven. Those are the terms, set by the one who died on a cross. But if you want Him to deal with them all, then look to that cross. Christ is the Savior of the world. Christ receives all who come to Him, red and yellow, black and white.

Does that sound too much like a trite children's song, the kind they used to sing in Sunday School back in the fifties? Better that than the howls of the inmates of the final asylum.

CHAPTER 4

THIS CRIMSON CARNAGE

This essay, which expands on some of the issues raised in the last chapter, was originally published on June 23, 2015, a week after nine people were killed and three injured in a shooting at the Emanuel African Methodist Episcopal Church in Charleston, South Carolina. All dates and data are from the original.

I begin by saying that I think of the American flag with affection, respect, and sorrow. I think of what it *used* to represent, what it *ought* to represent, and what it periodically still represents. The sorrow has to do with what our ruling elites are insisting that it must *come* to represent, and the grief is over their many successes in that endeavor. Despite this, I do not yet believe the American flag is a lost cause. Take that as the starting point.

But if our rule in these matters must be the logic of those demanding that any and all vestiges of the Confederacy come down, we will soon enough discover that this is a knife that can cut in all kinds of directions. In all of this, the issue is not so much what you do as *why* you are doing it. If you admit a false principle into the settlement of public disputes like this one—and I hate to be the one to bring you the sorrowful tidings—*the false principle does not disappear when the dispute does*. It remains there, propped up in the corner, cocked and loaded, waiting for the next dispute. And because of the times we live in, there *will* be a next dispute, probably in about three weeks. Glad to see she was among those who could make it.

None of this has anything whatever to do with a desire for a do-over at Gettysburg. I am carrying no water for a neo-Confederate anything. If you think I am, then that simply means that you are not grasping a point that is dangerous to miss. I am not fighting yesterday's battles. I am fighting today's battles and some of tomorrow's. If you want me to believe that the Confederate flag in South Carolina should come down because of sins x, y, and z, then I am simply inquiring why another flag should not come down because of far more heinous sins X, Y, and Z. Don't accuse me of racialist sins I have despised all my life, and then call me stupid. Answer the question. I've got all day.

And it won't do to say that the American flag is the flag of an extant power, an actual country, because that just means that application of this grand principle might take some actual courage. If you refrain because fighting adversaries who are armed and dangerous is . . . well, dangerous, then you are exactly the kind of person who would have played it safe in 1850. People kept their heads down then too.

Let me explain what I mean, and I want to ask you to hear me out.

In 1969, the baseball hero Jackie Robinson said this about the American flag in an interview with the *New York Times*. "I wouldn't fly the flag on the Fourth of July or any other day ... When I see a car with a flag pasted on it, I figure the guy behind the wheel isn't my friend."

This is not the moment to whitesplain to Jackie that this feeling would be appropriate with symbols that were used to oppress his people a century and a half ago, but is not appropriate with regard to what he thinks of as oppression right now. I would want to differ with Robinson's course of action, because we see things differently. But if we have already admitted the principle that what matters is his feelings and not the facts as understood and processed by millions of other people and scores of subcultures, where are we?

The problem applies to both flags, simply on the basis of the history of race relations as *normally* understood. But let us apply additional biblical standards to the situation and see what happens.

From the adoption of the Constitution in 1789 to the outbreak of hostilities in 1861, the American flag flew over race-based chattel slavery, constitutionally recognized. That was 72 years. The *Roe v. Wade* decision happened in 1973, wrapped up in penumbral evasions and lies, but still done in the name of the Constitution, the flag of which is Old Glory. That means that abortion has been a settled constitutional right for 42 years now. In another 30 years we will have been chopping babies up in the name of the Constitution for as long as blacks were bought and sold under the aegis of the Constitution.

And screw this into your minds—our treatment of the unborn is far, far worse than slavery was and involves many more millions of people.

> As a cage is full of birds, so are their houses full of deceit: therefore they are become great, and waxen rich. They are waxen fat, they shine: yea, they overpass the deeds of the wicked: they judge not the cause, the cause of the fatherless, yet they prosper; and the right of the needy do they not judge. (Jer. 5:27–28)

If there is one cause we have absolutely refused to hear, it is the cause of the fatherless.

Since the shooting in Charleston last week, approximately 15,000 children have lost their lives in this country; legally, according to the nine black-robed Nazgul; safely, at least if you don't count the baby; but scarcely rarely. Blacks make up about thirteen percent of the general population, and yet are represented in about 35 percent of the abortions. That is disproportionate enough *to lean genocidal*, and to make it the actual legacy of the very white bones of Margaret Sanger. That means 5,250 of these children, slaughtered legally *since just last Wednesday*, were black. Who speaks for them? I don't count because I have a picture of Stonewall Jackson in my office.

Isn't that the limit? I have spoken out repeatedly against this racial monstrosity from my enclave here in Sherwood Forest, while most of the Big Voices for Racial Reconciliation cannot be persuaded to give a tinker's damn about it. John Piper, God bless him forever, is an exception. When it comes to this subject, President Obama is a partial birth abortion ghoul and a large number of people from the soft evangelical middle voted for him. *Twice.* But what did they vote for when they did that? They voted for the continuation of a policy that on average takes one out of every four black Americans out of line and kills him dead. And everybody who voted for Obama, white or black, voted for *that* and ought to retire from lecturing anybody else over race relations ever again.

The 15,000, white and black, who have lost their lives since last week do not have any makeshift memorials springing up anywhere. No flowers propped against fences and no teddy bears left for the nameless. Nobody in any position of significant influence speaks for them with any kind of moral authority. But since we are talking about *racial* justice here, let us just address that aspect of our national tragedy. Since *Roe*, about 13 million black children have been executed. *Thirteen million.* That is more than the total population of Hawaii, Idaho, Maine, New Hampshire, Mississippi, New Mexico, and Nebraska. So black lives matter, do they? And coming back to the point, what flag flew over the courthouses that continue to authorize this crimson carnage? What flag was still flying there just this morning? How many more decades before the great principle of flag indignation kicks in? Would the populations of ten more Midwestern states do it? It took Hitler only twelve years to ruin the swastika forever. How many years do we get?

So when I move from the shooting in Charleston to abortion, *I am not changing the subject.* We are talking race-based murder in both instances. Thirteen million. It appears plain to me that some folks don't want a future for black people, and it also appears to me that a lot of other well-placed people are prepared to let them run with that plan. Are you one of them? If you tripped and fell over my earlier statement about Stonewall, then perhaps it is because you are more concerned about a gnat in north Idaho than about the caravan of camels that our evangelical leadership specializes in swallowing.

Some Christians have not realized the magnitude of the problem because the unborn have no voice. They really are defenseless. But in the Bible, innocent blood cannot really be silenced because whenever it is shed it cries out from the ground. In our case, it cries out from the polished linoleum floors of our abortion mills. God is just and will not be mocked. We *will* reap what we have sown, and our only possible refuge from righteous judgment over the blood we have shed is in the righteous blood that Pilate shed.

If the men of Sodom can rise up to condemn Capernaum, then the men of old Charleston can rise up at the day of resurrection and condemn us. They did things that appall us, true enough, and we are right to be appalled. But we do things that would appall them and they would have every right to be even more appalled.

John Rawls once said that your concept of the ideal society should be constructed without you knowing where you were going to be born into that society. This is just one more variation on the Golden Rule, and by this measure, if you were going to be conceived as the child of black parents in North America, would you prefer Charleston in 1850 or Chicago in 2015? I know which one involves a certified nurse counting up all your pieces so that they can make sure they throw *all* of you away. Be honest. Be brutally honest, and in the light of that honesty I would then invite you to rethink everything you thought you knew about racial reconciliation. You are not living in the kind of country you thought you were, and the myths you were taught about our recent history are just laughing at you behind your back.

The only way the *ethnoi* can be reconciled to one another is through the blood and water that came out of Jesus' side. But if we go this route, we must teach the nations to obey *all* that Jesus taught. That means His Word is authoritative over everything, and He wants His people to do far better with racial reconciliation than to be MSNBC's echo chamber. A good start in racial reconciliation would be for everyone to start loving the truth more than we love flattery.

All this said, I know that the Confederate battle flag has been used in some awful ways, and if we are speaking the truth we must include that one. By now the families of the Charleston victims must have seen photos online of their assailant brandishing one. Their feelings about it are completely justifiable, period, stop. Our task there is simply to weep with those who weep. My task is simply to ache with them as my brothers and sisters, pray for them, and do my level best not to compound their grief.

In addition, I have white friends whose "unreconstructed" days really were mixed in with racism and bigotry, and their way out does need to be repentance and walking away. I have no quarrel with any of this.

But the one thing we will not be allowed to walk away from is *the strategy that is being run on us.* As Trotsky put it, "You may not be interested in war, but war is interested in you." That is something we must come to understand. The people behind all our symbol controversies are the same people. Their fellow travelers change, as do their tools and patsies, but they are relentless about the same thing over and over again. They say that a "heritage not hate" sticker really "is too" hate. But do you really want to put *them* in charge of what is "really hate"? They are the same people who say that bakers who will only put hetero figurines on top of their cakes are driven by hate, too.

So while we labor at all these things, we have to remember this is one screwed up planet, and consequently the same sort of thing can be said (legitimately) of virtually any other symbol. It is even true of the cross. Do you have a cross in your sanctuary? Try showing a picture of that cross to the father of a bride whose wedding was blown up in Yemen by a wayward drone, sent to him by the "crusaders," the Americans.

The reply comes back that the cross has an important and necessary meaning that is not contaminated by those mistakes and abuses, and the Confederate flag only means KKK rallies and redneck drinking parties. What needful meaning could possibly be there? Said the people who are just days away from the Supreme Court mandating same-sex mirage for all fifty states, which states will all put up with it docilely even though the overwhelming majority of them don't want anything of the kind.

We badly need a doctrine of the lesser magistrates and a robust understanding of nullification, and we need a symbol for it. Now I would be happy for the battle flag to go into the history books. Let us make way for a new symbol of resistance to federal tyranny. What do you suggest?

A fighting gerbil on a yellow background? Like a kinder, gentler Gadsden flag, one that won't be so off-putting?

Whatever symbol it is, our adversaries will see to it that it will be identified with racism in about ten minutes. That is precisely what happened with the Gadsden flag at Tea Party rallies. Here was a movement dedicated to the most nonracial thing ever—basic budgetary math—and they were immediately assaulted for their *racism*. Whatever flag you pick, they will demand that you make it small enough that they can't see it. And then they will accuse you of a microaggression with your microflag. They have been running this play enough times that we really ought to recognize it by now. The play is this—*they must be put in charge of all definitions.* And my response to that is, let me think about it, no.

None of this is said in defense of continuing the serious use of the flag as a symbol of resistance. It does have a lot of baggage. But because I acknowledge this, I am then accused of inexplicable foot-dragging. Just take it down, man! But what I am acknowledging is a history of *sin*. See my essays in *Black and Tan*, particularly the chapter addressing what it means to be "regenerate but unreconstructed." I believe that every Christian should always be prepared to confess sin, biblically defined. What I am rejecting is *demonization*. And to simply go along with what they are currently demanding is to help establish their authority to demonize. I don't want to accede control of that process to them. I don't want them to have the demonization gun—I know where they are going to point it next.

So I do want to replace the flag, but I don't want to do it in a way that enthrones totalitarians, giving them complete control over our dictionary of symbols. These are the people who don't know the difference between boys and girls. These are the people who fiercely condemn female circumcision in Saudi Arabia and applaud genital mutilation by another name in California. These are the people who are willing to call people racists if they want to spend less than we take in. So mark me down as happy to replace the flag—but I just don't want to replace it with a white one. And I understand the rainbow is taken.

In the meantime, the kind of Christian leader who gets worked up over a decal on a pick-up truck belonging to the sort of good old boy who spends half of every paycheck at Cabela's, but who has no visceral reaction whatever to that big Planned Parenthood logo which he drives by every day, where *today's* horrors are actually being perpetrated, is not, apart from repentance, going to be part of the reformation we so desperately need.

And last, in writing all this, I should say I am not worried about forfeiting any choice invitations to the great banquet of Reformed evangelicalism. I wasn't really getting those anyway. Having spent half my life knee-deep in opprobrium, I might as well use the peculiar advantage afforded by such a situated perspective to do what Arthur Koestler once advised: "One should either write ruthlessly what one believes to be the truth, or else shut up." Having done so, I will now shut up.

CHAPTER 5

PRETTY SURE
IT IS NOT YOU

Flannery O'Connor wrote that everything that rises must converge, but this must also be said of everything that is circling the drain. The shared worldview of our chattering classes appears to me to be nothing more than a vast epistemic sinkhole. This is the kind of thing that could make Turretin, were he present with us, exclaim something like *zut alors!* which, when translated, means something like *holy smokes*. You know, a little inside term of art from one of the great scholars of the Reformation.

In order to be cast as a radical or a crazy these days, all you need do is say something like "A man should be judged by the content of his character, and not by the color of his skin." Total wingnuttery. If you insist on equal weights and measures, no thumb on the scale, whether that thumb be black like Al Sharpton's or white like David Duke's, or Daisy Duke's, for that matter, if you maintain something along the lines of "all thumbs matter," as in, keep *any* kind of thumb off the scale, you will be written off as a crackpot or, as the professionals would call it, a psychoceramic.

I mean, how dare you say that we should cultivate an official cultural color blindness? I know that it is ostensibly the stated goal and everything, but if anyone hazards to suggest that we actually give it a try, they will be grabbed where the pants hang loose and frog-marched to the curb.

I say all this because I wroted something that hit a nerve, and I was kind of surprised by the nerve it hit. I know, I shouldn't be surprised by anything anymore, but I kind of was.

Following the August 2015 shooting of Alison Parker and Adam Ward, I tweeted, "So a black guy shot some white people to start a race war. What flag do we have to take down that will fix it this time?"

What was that about? You should recall that after the Charleston shootings a few months earlier, after what seemed like minutes, a hue and holler went up about how we needed to take down the Confederate flag from its place on the grounds of the South Carolina capital. A full-court press was called, and there we were. Dylann Roof, who shot the people in that church, was a white punk who wanted to start a race war. It wasn't long before pictures of him brandishing the Confederate flag appeared online, and see? See?

No, I don't see. The problem is not race. The problem is *godlessness*. The problem is not that our society is racially divided. The problem is that we are divided from *God*, estranged from Him.

And now, in circumstances so close as to be almost a parody, a black man shoots a couple of white people on live television because he wanted to start a race war too. And since flags appear to be a necessary part of this kind of thing, a rainbow flag was found in Vester Flanagan's apartment. The pretend solution to these horrific crimes is to go in big for empty gestures, and so let us call for evenhandedness in our distribution of empty gestures. What flag do we have to take down now that will fix everything? Flanagan was homosexual, and he had a culprit flag in his apartment....

But lo, my observation caused sadness on the Internet. No, not the kind of sadness that Frodo had while going to the Grey Havens, or the kind that Treebeard had while marching on Isengard. He was, as you recall, "sad, but not unhappy." No, I made some people both sad and unhappy.

@douglaswils lost of respect for you I expected more.[1]

@douglaswils What a personally irresponsible and pastorally inept thing to say. Highly inappropriate.[2]

@douglaswils I'm really sorry a flag is such a big issue for you, Doug. Would you like to talk about it?[3]

@douglaswils what did Paul say? Something about "not all tweets beneficial?" Seems appropriate here.[4]

1. Jesse David (@JesseDavidW), Twitter, April 22, 2015, 11:10 a.m., https://twitter.com/JesseDavidW/status/636989504818126848.
2. Ryan Burton King (@RyanBurtonKing), Twitter, August 27, 2015, 10:49 a.m., https://twitter.com/RyanBurtonKing/status/636958648556724224.
3. Wesley McLachlan (@wesmac5), Twitter, April 22, 2015, 8:08 a.m., https://twitter.com/wesmac5/status/636918208541364224.
4. Tweet no longer available.

@douglaswils What a ridiculous thing to say, Doug.
You know it's bigger than that. Why say something so
incendiary?[5]

Of course it is bigger than that. Double standards always are. Hypocrisy is always much bigger than the sin it
pretends not to be committing. Liars hate being caught. It
throws them off their rhythm.

Look. We live in a generation when Democratic can-
didates can be hounded off a stage simply for saying "all
lives matter," which is apparently a racist dog whistle to
the incoherent and jumbled jive-mongers, who demand
that "black lives matter" be the only official chant, and
these pasty white politicians cannot even defend themselves by pointing out their own obvious hypocrisies. "No,
no, please don't run me off stage. I clearly don't believe
it. I am still in favor of selling black baby parts to white
researchers. And I promise to adhere to the 'black lives
matter' shibboleth simultaneously, while simpering and
groveling throughout, all while voting for continued millions to subsidize the merchandising of a disproportionate
number of black baby organs. We have to keep the sale of
dead black babies affordable for the important white researchers. Otherwise because racism!"

If you cannot make any sense out of the standards at
play in the previous paragraph, I think you can relax because I don't think it is you.

5. Griffin Gulledge (@griffingulledge), Twitter, April 22, 2015, 8:04 a.m.,
https://twitter.com/griffingulledge/status/636917313313337344.

CHAPTER 6

SKINISM

One collection of folks who excel at both racial vainglory and racial animosity is a group that call themselves *kinists*. I call them *skinists*.

I take it as a given that any conservative Christian who addresses cultural issues at all is not worth his salt if he does not get himself accused of racism. I am convinced that unless we are drawing that charge somehow, some way, then we are not doing our part to threaten the prevailing multicultural hooey. It is therefore important to incur the charge of racism. It is equally important that the charge be a slander and a falsehood.

Sometimes the liars on the left start to believe their own propaganda and cannot fathom why I would be in a conflict or dispute with any kind with racist. The answer is very simple really. Their leftist propaganda is false, and racism is not a sin against the state, or the people, or the prevailing leftist sensibilities. Racial malice and racial vainglory are sins against God, not because they take the obvious factors of race into account as they interpret the world, but because they are malicious and vainglorious.

Cultures can be sinful or righteous, good or evil, orderly or chaotic, advanced or primitive, rich or poor. But all of them are a product of a people's *cultus*—they are a function of the god or God they worship, and not a function of the God who made them. The thing that requires me to identify kinists as racist (and as much in defiance of the Scriptures as any they oppose) is the overt malevolence they routinely show toward the image and work of God Himself. To mock folly and sin is a prophetic duty. To mock the color of a man's skin is to defy the handiwork of God. Crimes motivated by racial animosity (in any direction) reveal a pathetic culture, the end result of worshipping pathetic gods. They were not the end result of the triune God's decision to make some of us white and some of us black. When whites worship pathetic gods, the end result features the same kind of twistedness. The issue for us as Christians is always worship. And how can these people say they love God, whom they have not seen, when they routinely taunt the handiwork of God in others, handiwork they have seen, thereby showing that they detest the image of God? Of course they might say they only mean to insult certain sins—they might say that in response, but it is not what they actually do. Spend fifteen minutes on a skinist website or Facebook group, and you will find plenty of examples of hostility to the creational work of God. If I were admonishing a man for laziness, and I suddenly found myself upbraiding him for having two legs, I have crossed over from legitimate admonition of a character deficiency into a critique of God's engineering skills. And if I cannot tell the difference between the two, I ought to shut up for a while. When men are attacked for being black, the attack is on Jesus Christ Himself—for He is the one who is the Creator of the black race, made in the image of God. But the response will come: "Lord, when did we attack and insult You . . . ?"

Imagine a great work of art that had been horribly vandalized by some deranged criminal. And suppose further a group of people were standing around looking at the damage. The different responses reveal the modern politics of race very well. One man says that he thinks the orange spray paint and razor action across the venerable Da Vinci canvas show the work of alternative genius, a primitive and authentic statement, a cry from the heart. This critic is a multiculturalist. Another fellow says that it is a darn shame about the vandalism and begins dusting for fingerprints. He is the normal one, a cop without any graduate credits in sociology. I want to be like that guy. But the third is the skinist. He starts going on and on about the awful vandalism and what a tragic loss it is. And thus far we agree, and for about ten minutes I think we are okay. But the more he talks, the more we hear him savaging aspects of the original painting. He is not praising the orange paint; he is damning the orange paint, and the original paint, and the canvas, and the horse it rode in on. He is the skinist. The first man praises the vandal and rejects the painter. The second man praises the painter and rejects the vandal. The third damns both the painter and the vandal.

The fifth commandment requires us to honor our father and mother, and Scripture is clear that a man is to take care of his own household first. If he does not, he is worse than an unbeliever. This responsibility works outward, in concentric circles. And I freely assert that honoring my father and mother brings with it a requirement to honor my people. These folks might want to say that makes me a kinist. No, not at all, and a moment's thought should reveal why.

To use the fifth commandment as a template for understanding this, the multiculturalist tries to instill respect for another man's mother by instilling contempt for one's own. The kinist tries to instill respect for one's own mother by instilling contempt for the mothers of those "others." In contrast to both, the biblical position is that it is precisely because I honor my own mother that I understand why another man is required by God to honor his.

But sin complicates things. To continue the illustration, not all mothers are equally venerable. This is why we must learn to preach the gospel to all, admonish all, identify sin in all, and in all this, sin is to be understood as the enemy of our true humanity in Christ. St. Peter tells us in unambiguous terms that we are to honor all men. But these people reserve to themselves the right to show contempt for men as men, under the guise of rebuking their sins, cultural or personal.

One of the awful things that is routinely done on skinist websites, in the name of sound theology and God's law, is to heap contempt on the work of God, the image of God. It is one thing to attack the work of the vandals—faithfulness requires it. And when you attack the vandals, the multicultural relativists will counterattack with their own spurious charges of racism. Fine, let them do so. But when these people enter the fray and start sniping at the original work of God as though that were part of the vandalism, the results are detestable. And this is a rebuke of their petty malevolence, which must be repented of. But I do not attribute their sin in this to the fact that God gave them ten toes, red hair, or a couple of kidneys.

In the midst of discussions about levels of crime among blacks, various handwringers and bedwetters want to simply believe the propaganda we are served constantly, which is fundamentally a message of denial. They want to say there no objective difference in how different racial groups in our nation behave. It reminds me of the joke about the drunk looking for his car keys under a street light, and when he is asked if that is where he lost them, he replies, "No, but the light is better here." For the sake of a superficial advantage (better light) he overlooks the obvious (which is that his keys are somewhere else). Just last week my wife and I were in an airport watching a frail little old lady in a wheel chair selected for the full tilt security treatment. Is she a Saudi terrorist? No, but the light is better here.

It also reminds me of Chesterton's observation that when confronted with the fact that a man can get real pleasure out of skinning a cat, the only two options are to deny the union between God and man, as the Christians do, or deny there is a God, as the atheists do. The new theologians, he said, think it a satisfactory solution to deny the cat. The pc crowd insist upon denying the cat, and if you press the point, they will blame the skinned cat on the fact that people like you press the point.

That said, why do I believe the kinists misrepresent the biblical gospel so frightfully? The kinists stumble at a fundamental point in biblical polemics. They apply their principles to *others* first. Jesus tells individuals to get the beam out of their own eye first. Then they will be able to see when they address others. Yourself first, others second. Paul says the same (Gal. 6:1): If someone is overcome in a trespass, the one who is spiritual should correct him, considering himself lest he also be tempted. And in Romans 2, Paul makes the same point with regard to the ethnic tensions between Jew and Gentile—he rebukes the Jews who put on airs with regard to their superiority to Gentiles when, he points out, they do the very same kind of thing.

In this spirit, I will believe that the kinists are not driven by racially based malice or vainglory (which is how I have defined racism) when they begin attacking the sins of their *own* people as the result of racially based predispositions. If blacks are predisposed to certain sins, then it follows that we should apply this standard to whites as well. But these are white people, kinists, wanting to address the ills our nation is facing. So why not do it by attacking those things we do *because we are white*? But they do not do this kind of thing at all, which means that they are operating a butcher's shop with one thumb on the scale.

What are the characteristic *white* sins? When you do the logic chopping thing, and carefully distinguish genetic determinism from genetic probabilism, but you do this only with all the *other* groups, there is a severe problem with spiritual dishonesty. Your own group is made up of sinners, certainly, but they are just people, you know? *We* sin because we are descended from Adam, and everybody is a sinner. *They* sin because they are descended from Adam *and* they are black. This is just atrocious.

I am of Scots and Scots-Irish descent. A great book on the contribution these people have made to our history is *Born Fighting* by James Webb. For sheer cussedness, there is no finer group anywhere. The gods they worshipped, and then the God they came to worship, along with many centuries of hardscrabble living, created a certain ethos that had specific and great strengths and some pretty crazy weaknesses. Psalm 115 makes clear that we become like the gods we worship, which is why I attribute the faults of black culture to their gods over the course of the last millennia. I do the same for whites, and for Asians, and so on. But I also acknowledge something of a hermeneutical spiral here. How does it come about that this group picks the cruel gods of war and that group picks the sensate gods of debauchery? There are racial differences when it comes to faults, and there are differences when it comes to virtues. And what will the gospel do? When the earth is full of the knowledge of the Lord as the waters cover the sea, what will Africa be like? The scriptural answer is that it will be glorious—and different. The gospel saves us, and glorifies us, without throwing us into an egalitarian blender.

We can hasten that day if we pay attention to our *own* faults and failings. The black "preachers" like Sharpton and Jackson are betraying their people because they will not confront their characteristic sins. In this, they are just like the skinists who will not confront characteristic white sins, petty racism being among them.

I mentioned in an earlier chapter the time I was talking to a black student's mother who was convinced that the other kids didn't like her son and that he was doing poorly in school because he was black. He was actually having trouble because he was a pill, but I granted the point to his mother. I told her that she believed her son lived in a world in which he would have to work twice as hard to get the same distance as some white kid. Now since that is the kind of world she believed he lived in, I needed to tell her that he was currently working half as hard. Given that, what did she think was going to happen to him? What happens to people who have to work twice as hard and they only work half as hard? They get chewed up and spit out. This mother needed to hear and understand these things (and she needed it desperately, for the sake of her son), but she couldn't really hear them from me. She needed to hear this kind of thing from the leaders of her people, so that she could really hear it.

I am a conservative white guy. I am Reformed and Calvinistic. I have a Celtic heritage. I am an evangelical. I am a preacher, called to attack sin. So whose sins should *I* attack? There are fireworks preachers out there who put on quite a display in the pulpit, always taking care to hammer the sins that are not being committed by the people actually present. Gather all the born-againers, and preach against the sins of secular humanists. The problem should be obvious. I will press the point home, and leave off, by telling the story of an old black preacher who preached on heaven and hell all the time, heaven and hell, heaven and hell. When he was asked why he did this, he replied that he *had* preached on chicken stealing once, but it had dampened the enthusiasm.

CHAPTER 7

PRIDE AND WHITE PRIVILEGE

One of the good things about controversy is that it makes you answer questions you wouldn't otherwise address, and it sometimes makes you answer uncomfortable ones. One question that has come up in response to my writing about racial justice has to do with the issue of "white privilege." How much do whites just take for granted, not knowing how different the same world looks to those who do not share in those privileges? That got me to thinking—and Wodehouse once said that certain minds are like the soup in a bad restaurant, better left unstirred—but here are the results of my musings anyhow.

It is easy for modern Christians to assume that privilege, while not exactly a sin, is closely related. Bigotry, prejudice, animosity, and malice would be the sins proper—spiritual diabetes—and basking thoughtlessly in your privileged status would be like being prediabetic. You aren't being bad *yet*, but you are in the danger zone. There is something to this, but the problem is that the spiritual precautions we take are usually in the wrong direction entirely—treating our prediabetes with Snickers bars. We tend to fortify ourselves with guilt over that privilege when we ought to be overflowing with gratitude. But this does require explanation.

There are many forms of privilege—wealth, education, birth order, race, looks, age, experience, intelligence, nationality, and so on. Not only that, but you can then start combining them—wealthy *and* intelligent *and* good-looking and so on. Some privileges are detachable, and others are dyed in the wool. The sins that afflict the privileged are many, but the central one would be pride, a sleek arrogance that feels that they somehow earned or merited the blessings that surround them. Born on third, as the saying goes, and they think they hit a triple. The sins that accompany the unprivileged are also many, but the central one would be resentful envy. This is the gnawing sensation in the gut, like a rat was living down there, that feels like it was *robbed*. Born on first, and they think they hit a triple.

But the Bible teaches us that every form of wealth and privilege we have should always call forth *gratitude*. If we have sin to confess in this regard, it should be the sin of pride, not the sin of privilege itself. There is no sin of privilege. If someone is insisting that I must repent of racial privilege, repent of the doors that are open to me because of the whiteness "that is invisible to me," I deny it. The *Bible* defines sin, not the envious race theories of others. But not only must I not be proud of whatever privileges I have, so also others must not envy them. And because there is always someone who has way more privileges than I do, I can check my heart by seeing if I am as glad for the privileges of those above me, as I am for my own.

Envious looks can be seen all the way up the ladder, and they are sinful all the way up.

But there is an important qualification here. We can't talk about this without talking about it, and we have to use the same vocabulary (privilege) in different areas, and that could trip us up. If someone accuses me of white privilege, and I own it as a form of *guilt*, then the envy games may continue. But if I regard it as a blessing from God for me (like all my privileges), then this could be immediately twisted into an accusation that I have embraced some grotesquery like "white pride," as though whiteness really is innately superior. I deny that—the privilege here comes from the culture and history of the thing, not from genetics. If I say I occupy a position of privilege in this culture because I am white (which is true enough), but I don't feel guilty over it, then it is assumed that I am trying to justify some form of soft racism, however mild it might come across to my fellow (privileged) whites, and however glaring it might appear to blacks. Not so.

It is true that white Americans have many privileges (most of which are invisible to them) over against what is experienced by African Americans. But there is no more sense in feeling guilty over this than there is in African Americans feeling guilty over *their* privileges measured against the average experience of African Africans. Look at the opportunities that President Obama has had over against his half-brother from Kenya. The Scriptures tell us what to do with such situations, which I will get to shortly.

"You don't know what it's like..." is how the complaint usually starts. This is self-evidently true, manifestly true. Yet the basic moral duty found in the Golden Rule requires a foundational empathy for others that has learned how to cross (after a fashion) the various barriers that divide us. Husbands are called to know and understand some aspect of what it is like to be a woman (Eph. 5:28–29; 1 Pet. 3:7). Believers are called to know and understand some fundamental aspect of what it is like to minister to some beat-up guy on the other side of a sharp ethnic divide (Luke 10:33). In these situations, the only reason why we wouldn't know "what it's like" to be in that other person's shoes would be because our consciences had been seared with a hot iron. A husband should be able to measure his response to his wife's headache by how he would like to be treated when he has one like that (Eph. 5:28–29). They both have heads. Both a white man and a black man can know what it would be like to be beat up and left by the side of the road, and so either of them can be summoned to the role of the Good Samaritan.

But there is another sense in which we cannot cross the divide. We cannot erase the privilege, and when we try, we only make things worse with our patronizing do-goodery. A beautiful woman cannot erase that privilege in her dealings with a plain woman. An educated man cannot erase that privilege in his dealings with an uneducated man. A wealthy man cannot erase that privilege in his dealings with a poor man. Even if he gave all his wealth away, which is the kind of thing that some rich guys do when they endow the monastery they are going to go live in, he is still the guy who did that.

So I cannot erase the color of my skin, or the position of privilege it gives me. It is what it is. Now what? What does obedience look like when you find yourself born into privilege? Go back to nonexistence and ask God for a do-over?

When those who are privileged are made to feel guilty for those privileges, especially the ones that cannot be altered, a scam is being run on them. They are being worked over by guilt so that they will be a softer touch when the right time comes. Those who work them over like this are the envious practitioners of *ressentiment*. But the real way out of the cycle of racial animosities is for the privileged to repent of every form of pride, and for those lacking those privileges to repent of every form of envy.

And here is where it gets sticky. I have been in various forms of "slavery controversies" for at least a decade, and one of the most striking things about these controversies is the blithe disregard many Christians have for the blunt and very clear teaching on the subject in the New Testament. I have referenced a clear set of verses repeatedly, and over those years not one of my accusers has sought to engage with the plain teaching of the Bible. It is like I have been citing invisiverses.

Let us assume that the privileges (and lack of them) that we are talking about are all directly downstream from the fact of centuries of slavery here in North America. If that is the case, then we can reason by analogy from these passages in order to see what we are called to do now, each in our respective positions. The only way these verses would not apply is if our current difficulties had nothing to do with slavery. But to say that gives up the central grievance, and to say that would also have the disadvantage of being untrue. So, what might our corporate sanctification look like?

"And, ye masters, do the same things unto them, forbearing threatening: knowing that your Master also is in heaven; neither is there respect of persons with him" (Eph. 6:9). Those Christians who were masters (a position of privilege) were not commanded to feel guilty about it. They were commanded to put it into perspective, and to remember that they too were under a Master in heaven, and to recall that their privileged status was going to *evaporate* at the Day of Judgment. Having gained the perspective of eternity, they were called to remember the laws of reciprocity in their treatment of those under their authority. In short, *they were commanded to love.*

> Let as many servants as are under the yoke count their own masters worthy of all honour, that the name of God and his doctrine be not blasphemed. And they that have believing masters, let them not despise them, because they are brethren; but rather do them service, because they are faithful and beloved, partakers of the benefit. These things teach and exhort. (1 Tim. 6:1–2)

Paul also teaches that those who were servants should honor their masters, and they should be doubly sure to do this if their masters were Christians. But whenever I have heard Christian masters referred to, it has been invariably for the sake of doubling the resentment, not doubling the honor. In short, slaves were *commanded to love.*

This is not the opiate of the masses. This is not propping up the structures of oppression with Bible verses. Love is the fastest and surest way out of every form of slavery, and it is the *only* way of escape from the vicious cycle of the racial animosities that continue to afflict us.

White Christians and black Christians must work together, and this means forgiving one another. Whites must forgive blacks, and blacks must forgive whites. Whites must seek forgiveness from blacks (for their sins as biblically defined) and blacks must seek forgiveness from whites (for their sins as biblically defined). And if your reaction is defensive, seeing the need to seek forgiveness as a burden that only that *other* group has (whichever one it is), then congratulations—*you* are the problem.

> As for the rich in this present age, charge them not to be haughty, nor to set their hopes on the uncertainty of riches, but on God, who richly provides us with everything to enjoy. They are to do good, to be rich in good works, to be generous and ready to share. (1 Tim. 6:17–18)

Those who are privileged are commanded not to be haughty, and to use their position of privilege in the service of others. They are to share what they have, not as though they are trying to be deloused (in order to give the lice to others), but rather because they are grateful, and they want to include others in the blessing.

"A sound heart is the life of the flesh: But envy the rottenness of the bones" (Prov. 14:30). "Wrath is cruel, and anger is outrageous; but who is able to stand before envy?"(Prov. 27:4). Envy is not the path away from slavery; it is another, more insidious form of slavery. Envy consumes the one given over to it—rottenness of the bones—but it can be formidable in the meantime—who can stand before it? But someone once wisely said that bitterness is like eating a box of rat poison and then waiting for the rat to die.

And I know that some might say that I have written all this from the safe and privileged position of a white, middle-class pastor in America. That is demographically true, but I have actually written this from another position of privilege entirely. I was privileged to grow up with parents who loved Jesus Christ, and one another, and us. I was privileged to grow up in a home where the authority of the Scriptures was absolute. It says what it says, and it records what it records for God's glory and for our good.

So I am not trying to be the white guy. This is just my best imitation of the apostle John—we should be doing what we have heard from the beginning, which is to love one another.

CHAPTER 8

FERGUSON, FREDDIE, AND PHILANDO

The deaths of Michael Brown, Eric Garner, Freddie Gray, Philando Castile, Alton Sterling, and other black men in encounters with police officers have churned up a steady stream of outrage in recent years.

SKIN AND BLOOD

As the 2014 events in Ferguson, Missouri, demonstrated, lawlessness dislocates everything in the system, up and down the entire line.

People are complicated, especially when they are in sin, and situations are complex. So when people make up their minds about a particular allegation based entirely on the color of the participants, they are establishing nothing other than their own disqualification for having anything whatever to do with the justice system, or anything whatever to say about the future of race relations in America.

There are more than enough confirmed instances of police misbehavior to have made it quite possible the Wilson/Brown incident could have been one of them. They are more than enough confirmed incidents of inner-city black thuggery to have made that a possibility, as well. To be trapped in the kind of emotional blinders so that they can only accuse in one direction, and only defend in the other, is to be trapped in sin.

But the mob is omnivorous, ravenous, and blind. Rage doesn't make sense—if it did, it wouldn't be rage. And when frustration explodes, it never erupts in rational ways. The mob at Ephesus had no idea what they were doing there or what the point actually was (Acts 19:32), but they were more than willing to yell enthusiastically for a couple of hours about it.

The one thing a sane society may not do is cater to the insanity, trying to split the difference. In this regard, the behavior of the authorities in Missouri has been idiotic, and the actions of the Justice Department have been despicable. This is not because Wilson could not possibly have been guilty—it is because anybody who expects due process to run smoothly with a mob outside burning the place down is someone who specializes in grand inversions.

The mob is more than willing to ignore the camels and riot over the gnats. You want to show your displeasure over a white cop abusing (and killing) a black man, and you want to do this by abusing hundreds of black men and women? Suit yourself, but I don't particularly care for your theories of social justice. Don't tell us that "black lives matter" while showing your utter contempt for black lives. Anyone who turns matters of justice over to a mob of any color is an enemy of truth. And anyone who appeases such mobs is not fit for governance.

You have a complaint about the irregularities in the case that came before the grand jury? But is there any possibility that the anger of the mob was responsible for it? Making the prosecutor have to go through the motions of a grand jury in order to try to appease and acquit at the same time? A rioting mob that demands the "right answer" will get one of two things. Either it will get that right answer, and we have what is called a lynching, or it will be thwarted in that right answer. If it is thwarted, it will be done through a courageous response, which we did *not* have in Missouri, or a cowardly and convoluted one, which we did. When that happens, race relations are further corrupted, and the cycle of sin continues.

A mob that can demand indictments is also a mob that can demand convictions. To take one compromised step in that direction is a very great cultural evil. It seems self-evident to me that every Christian really ought to hate it—in his bones—whenever a crowd takes up a chant with a crucifixion theme in it. And we ought to hate it even if the object of their hatred is named Barabbas.

One last thing. Those soft evangelicals who spent their energy in this unhappy business trying to empathize with the rage of the crowd were undercutting the only possibility of hope. What every sinner in this tangled affair needed, whether white or black, is a once-for-all sacrifice. Other victims, whether guilty or not, will be brought to the altar in vain.

The only proclamation that can successfully interrupt this downward spiral of racial animosity is the death and resurrection of Jesus Christ. When in our blindness and folly we join the ultimate mob and cry out for His blood to be on us and on our children, God's gracious response looked far beyond our putrefying hatreds. He does apply that blood to us, but not for condemnation. He applies that blood to us so that a white man and a black man might *together* put on the new man:

> And have put on the new man, which is renewed in knowledge after the image of him that created him: Where there is neither Greek nor Jew, circumcision nor uncircumcision, Barbarian, Scythian, bond nor free: but Christ is all, and in all. Put on therefore, as the elect of God, holy and beloved, bowels of mercies, kindness, humbleness of mind, meekness, longsuffering; Forbearing one another, and forgiving one another, if any man have a quarrel against any: even as Christ forgave you, so also do ye. (Col. 3:10–13)

And to be baptized into that body is to be taken completely out of the mob.

SO THE PUNK IS NEW YORK CITY

In December 2014, a Staten Island grand jury decided not to indict officer Daniel Pantaleo for the July death of Eric Garner. On the surface, the situation in Staten Island and Ferguson—two instances of a grand jury's refusing to indict a white cop for the death of a black man—are quite similar. But other than that one factor, the situations are dramatically different. Actually, there is one other significant similarity—Al Sharpton is busy hustling for his bitterness business in both situations, and for him that particular business is always brisk. But with those similarities aside, I want to point to the stark difference for a moment.

This is not a trifle. Our ability to see the difference is the measurement of whether we are prepared to think biblically about race in America—and all the early returns indicate that we are nowhere close to ready.

As a preface to what I'm going to say, I want to note that it is perfectly reasonable to call upon the prosecutor in this case to do what was done in Ferguson, which is to release the evidence that was presented to the grand jury, which they apparently found so compelling. I say this because this could conceivably be a case where Proverbs 18:17 pulls a rabbit out of a hat, but it is awfully hard to see how that could happen. This whole Eric Garner mess appears to have all the characteristics of a travesty.

That said, I want to state my point near the very beginning so that if someone wants to get mad, they can start in on it now. Anyone who cannot see past the "refusal to indict" and "white cop/black victim" is an essential part of the problem. Anyone who links Ferguson and Staten Island as parallel situations is living out the very antithesis of King's dream—"the content of their character" is trumped, always and everywhere, by the presence of melanin.

And anybody who says that "white people don't get it" is an essential part of the problem. The fact is that white people who know what justice is do in fact "get it." White people who don't know what justice is don't get it. The same goes for black people who know what justice is, and again for those who don't know what justice is. Knowing how justice is supposed to work is not a function of skin pigmentation.

Think about this for just a few moments. What were Michael Brown and Eric Garner doing moments before they died? Hint: they both were involved with tobacco. Michael Brown was robbing a shopkeeper, walking out of a store with somebody else's cigars. He was being a punk, a thug. Eric Garner was selling loose cigarettes, which meant tax-free cigarettes. He was interrupted by the police, because New York City insists on having a piece of that action. Eric Garner was not being a punk; New York City was being a punk.

When Michael Brown was stopped by Darren Wilson, he was stopped *by a police officer who was doing exactly what a police officer ought to be doing*—in this case, following up on a reported theft. When Eric Garner was stopped by cops, he was being stopped by representatives of an officious and busypants nanny state, doing exactly what cops ought *not* to be doing. This is the same kind of thing that could have happened to someone being arrested for selling illegal Big Gulps.

I know why theft is against the law. Why is it against the law to sell cigarettes this way? When you multiply petty laws you are simply multiplying opportunities for contempt for the law to grow. And the more you multiply petty laws, the more the leeches in charge will feel like they have the right to "crack down on" those scofflaws who have managed to hang on to some of their own money. This was bad, but at least we aren't using SWAT teams to deal with cigarette vendors. Or armored assault vehicles. Yet.

And so now the problem is that the feds are coming in to fix everything. But they have already demonstrated their incompetence to deal with this kind of thing by their shameless pandering in the Ferguson situation. To add to the Tom Wolfe *Bonfire of the Vanities* atmosphere of everything, you have Al Sharpton parading back and forth like a rooster with an attitude, not to mention major tax liabilities. But the only real access the feds have to the situation is by making it a civil rights issue. That means they have to racialize it whether or not it had anything to do with race. They have the right to investigate it only if they prejudge it.

But suppose Eric Garner was not taken down for the color of his skin. Suppose he was taken down because he was trying to do something he should have had every right to do. Suppose the problem there was not race, but a soft despotism that wants to tax the air you breathe. Suppose that Michael Brown had been a big Bulgarian, and he wound up just as dead. But all this is to suppose that the official media narrative on all this is dead wrong.

Take note. All the people who will take charge of this investigation in order to ensure that justice is done don't appear to have the faintest idea what that word means.

A SHAKEDOWN GONE WRONG

Well, you can't say that NYC doesn't know how to make it worse. Ramsey Orta, the man who took the footage of Eric Garner's arrest and death, has been indicted on a gun charge.

In response to my point in the previous post, someone answered my question about what Brown and Garner were both doing moments before their deaths. My answer had to do with the stealing and selling of tobacco. Their answer was that both men were "resisting arrest." Quite, but even here the differences remain dramatic.

One was resisting arrest for theft, an offense recognized as socially actionable throughout the history of the whole world. The other was being harassed over violation of an imbecile law. And when you have a host of imbecile laws, you will have a host of confrontations that should never have been. This was one of them, and the fault lies squarely at the feet of those overlords in charge of "eating out our substance." The bloated state *always* needs cash, and this was nothing but a raw shakedown. Brown was a thief, just like NYC.

In NYC's defense, they were a thief who didn't intend to kill anybody. Sometimes the shakedown goes wrong, and somebody dies. My suggestion, as mild as it might be, is that they quit the shakedowns.

Here are Eric Garner's last words:

> Every time you see me, you want to mess with me. I'm tired of it. It stops today .... I'm minding my business, officer, I'm minding my business. Please just leave me alone. I told you the last time, please just leave me alone. Please. Please, don't touch me. Do not touch me .... I can't breathe. I can't breathe. I can't breathe ....

Contrast this with Brown's aggressive hostility to a policeman who was doing exactly what Charles Barkley knows—unlike other people I could mention—just what policemen ought to be doing.

Also, for the race-baiters, try to keep in mind that the officer in charge of the arrest was a black woman, a datum that conveniently does not show up in the footage you are seeing. This was not a racial incident. This was a different kind of outrage.

It was a travesty; it was a deadly farce. And it *is* a systemic problem, but it is not the systemic problem that everybody is yelling about.

ARMS FULL OF JUSTICE SWAG

In light of the events in Baltimore following Freddie Gray's April 2015 death, everyone wanted to have an honest conversation about race. The difficulty is that in honest conversations about race, nobody is allowed to say anything that is true. We have gotten to the point where the simple truth is inflammatory. Now the obvious truth should be about as inflammatory as a CVS pharmacy, but unfortunately, the logic of that observation is now officially running in the wrong direction.

So allow me, if you will, to say some things that I believe to both true and relevant. Here are seven observations related to race relations and public order that I wrote a couple of weeks after Gray's death. The date references are unchanged:

1. Some of my compatriots on the pasty end of the color spectrum start to panic whenever I write about race. They believe that I am not helping and that whatever I have to say will be detrimental to race relations within the body of Christ. But the black brothers in Christ that I count as friends don't feel the same way. They are not obligated to believe what I say, but I do want them to feel an obligation to believe that I am saying nothing other than what I believe to be true—and that that is the only reason I am saying it. Too many trendy evangelicals, if politically correct sentiments were water, act like those long-range lawn sprinklers, the ones that have a 360-degree reach. When my black friends

read what I say, they know that I believe what I am saying. When a pale fellow, pale both ways, gives them various Jessefied CNN talking points, they are never sure. So if you really want an honest conversation about race, stop saying what you are expected to say, and start saying what you actually think. That's what honesty means, incidentally.

2. The inner city pathologies that were on display in Baltimore are religious and cultural, not genetic or racial. We are observing one more failure of socialism, and not the failure of black people. As Iowahawk put it in a magnificent observation, "In 1959, Detroit was the wealthiest city in America and Cuba was the wealthiest country in Latin America. #HappyMayDay"[1] If you want to get the same pathologies we are seeing here, only with white people, that is perfectly possible. We have the technology. I recommend Theodore Dalrymple's *Life at the Bottom*[2] if you are up for a real eye-opener. The Baltimore riots do invite judgment, but make sure you triple-check the identity of the defendant. The defendant is leftism.

3. Scripture says that the sins of some men go before them, and others come behind. "Some men's sins are open beforehand, going before to judgment; and some men they follow after" (1 Tim. 5:24). As it happens, when a black idiot runs out of a store with his arms full of justice swag, his sin goes before him. When a white idiot, ensconced in his think tank at Harvard, proposes that we make everyone healthy, wealthy, and wise by federal fiat, his sin comes behind him.

---

1. David Burge (@iowahawkblog), Twitter, May 1, 2015. Tweet no longer available.
2. *Life at the Bottom: The Worldview That Makes the Underclass* (Chicago, IL: Ivan R. Dee, 2001).

Some men carry their sin in front of them like a shield, and others drag it behind them, like a rope. With some men, we see the consequences of the sin right away. With others, we don't see it for a good seventy-five years, and even then there is debate among the learned. So Baltimore is not what happens when blacks govern themselves. Baltimore is what happens when anybody governs according to the pious platitudes of the whitest people in New England.

4. If cops murdered Freddie Gray, and if the sufficient evidence is discoverable, then of course those cops should be charged, convicted, and punished. But whether any such evidence is extant will not be determined by how many bags of Doritos you manage to carry away from a burning store. When it comes to the administration of justice, mobs on the streets are, *um*, rarely helpful.

5. If there was a rush to indict these six cops in order to restore order, that means there will be the same kind of pressure to convict, in order to prevent Baltimore going up in a sheet of flame. You have created a circumstance where issues other than simple innocence or guilt are affecting what is going on in the courtroom. That is a terrible situation to be in. But at the same time, if there was a rush to indict, then the chances are also increased that the assembled cases were hurried and sloppy, and there may well be charges dropped later, or acquittals. When that happens—well, as we used to say in the Navy, stand by for heavy rolls.

6. When people live under a despotic tyranny, it is not surprising when they finally get to a breaking point. But that is not what this is. If this really were a "we're not going to take it anymore" moment, the mobs would be attacking police stations and city halls. The fact that they are

attacking innocent merchants is damning. What it means is that the rioters of Baltimore are publicly saying that in order to ruin somebody's life in this city, you need have no due process at all. You do not need evidence, you do not need a trial, you do not need justice. All you need is a grievance. But once you adopt that as your categorical imperative—so behave that you are willing for your behavior to become a universal law—you discover that the cops are allowed, under your new universal law, to have a grievance against men like Freddie Gray.

In short, the cops in this case might have a contempt for the demands of justice. The looters—sorry, undocumented shoppers—definitely have a contempt for the demands of justice. They are thus, demonstrably, the last people in the world we should listen to. They have voted for exactly the kind of government they claim they live under.

7. I mentioned inner city pathologies earlier. The central pathology there is fatherlessness. That pathology exists because progressive governments have declared war on fatherhood. They hate it, but when they have succeeded in virtually exterminating it, they find that a lot more police work is necessary. But you can't hire enough cops to contain a nation of fatherless men.

If you want flourishing cities, then there are two things that are necessary, two places to begin. You have to stop paying single moms to refuse to marry the fathers of their children, and you have to stop chasing jobs for those fathers out of the city with your regulations, taxes, rules, social engineering, and all-around fussy whiteness—because, let us be frank, your officious willingness to mess around with other people's lives is whiter than Woodrow Wilson's thighs.

CHAPTER 9

DIRTY COPS AND DUE PROCESS

E veryone knows that dirty cops exist. We all know that somewhere, somehow, some cops are on the take, some are morally incompetent, some are on a power trip, some disable their bodycams before taking care of business, and so on. Anyone who believes that dirty cops *can't* exist is someone who is unaware of the biblical doctrine of sin, is bereft of common sense, and is woefully lacking in his knowledge of the corpus of the American film industry.

So when an incident happens somewhere, one involving a cop and a black teenager, and all hell breaks loose, how are we supposed to think about it biblically? What are we to think of it while the rioting is in process? Since we know *a priori* that official malfeasance is a possibility, and even more likely in some corrupt jurisdictions, does this move everything to that famous "level playing field"? *No.*

Before there is an investigation, we don't know all the facts. Neither side knows all the facts. Those rioting don't know the facts, and those not rioting don't know the facts. Does this put both sides on an equal footing, then? *No.*

In the world of biblical justice, a mastery of the facts is necessary *in order to condemn.* The principle is stated over and over again in Scripture—"At the mouth of two witnesses, or three witnesses, shall he that is worthy of death be put to death; but at the mouth of one witness he shall not be put to death" (Deut. 17:6). You may not condemn a man unless his crime has been independently confirmed. Without such independent confirmation, you may not condemn a man for violating his responsibilities as a citizen, and you may not condemn an officer for an abuse of his powers. In the name of Christ, *you may not.*

The cops don't get to do it to us, and we don't get to do it to the cops.

It is biblically nonsensical to say that you need two or three witnesses in order to *not* condemn a man. To put it that way would amount to saying that a man is guilty unless he comes up with two or three witnesses who prove him not to be. That is, guilty unless proven innocent.

So prior to an investigation and trial, *nobody* has all the facts. But that still doesn't put everyone in the same position.

I don't need all the facts in order to *not* execute an accused officer. I need all the facts to condemn him. I don't need all the facts before I decline to burn down the shop of a Vietnamese immigrant. I don't need all the facts before I *don't* throw a brick through a window. I don't need all the facts before refusing to tip over a car to set it on fire.

DIRTY COPS AND DUE PROCESS

Before taking any action that would condemn or destroy someone or would destroy his property—before the use of coercion, in other words—I must know what actually happened. Otherwise I am just part of what John Knox once called "that rascal multitude."

When there is *prima facie* evidence of wrong, there should be an indictment. After the indictment, there should be a trial in open court, with the accused going into the trial with the presumption of innocence.

Take the rioting in Baltimore after Freddie Gray died in police custody. Millions of dollars went up in smoke because lots of people knew what happened, or so they thought. After the smoke cleared and charges were brought by the prosecutor against six cops, what happened? One acquittal after another. And how does one undo devastating riots?

The riots in Milwaukee following the August 2016 police shooting of Sylville Smith played out with a sickening familiarity. We don't need no stinking facts.

The people who know what side they are on before the trial, the people who don't *need* a trial to find out what they ardently feel about it, the people who justify rioting, *these* are the people that the Lord is visiting upon us for our chastisement.

As I learned growing up, having been taught by sane people, racism is the false belief that one race is inherently and essentially superior to another. Taken this way, and when the attitude is combined with malice, we can see that racism is a very grievous sin. God hates it, and one of the things Jesus came to do was eradicate that sin.

A lesser sin, but still a sin, is when the false belief of racial superiority is combined, not with malice, but with a patronizing do-goodery. Many missionaries from previous eras fell into this problem. We see a continuation of this variant of racism in affirmative action policies—policies quite effective in casting a shadow over every genuine black achievement. This highlights yet another destructive aspect of the "soft bigotry of low expectations." Because the apostles of uplift have snow-white motives, their racist assumptions are invisible to them. They would never use the phrase "white man's burden," but they operate in terms of it all the time. They are not racists, they claim, because they intend only good things for those lesser breeds without the law. And of course, they would never dream of expressing their smug superiority through phrases from Kipling. They express their smug superiority in other ways. Can racists be cowed? Sure. If an outcry is raised against either kind of racism, it can be successfully chased indoors. People still harbor their racist notions, and occasionally something will slip out, but for the most part they keep their racism to themselves. They stuff it. It is still in there somewhere, and God sees it, but for the most part nobody else does. If this kind of pressure is kept up, such unarticulated racism can morph into what is called white privilege, which in another time would simply have been called bad manners. We are now down to the level of what are called microaggressions. The political correctness police are out in force, calling everyone on every expression of what they consider to be such white privilege. Unfortunately, they wind up policing a good deal more.

This is not to say that there are no people who could personally benefit from that exercise that is quaintly called "checking your privilege." There are some insufferable bores out there, and there are people who puff themselves up like a barn owl when it is ten below. That is a problem, but, as mentioned above, it is a problem of manners.

Let me use an outrageous example. If we gave campus cops the authority to write up, at will, any student who spoke a sentence that did not have an appropriate subject-verb agreement, and there would be no possibility of appealing such a ticket, and no defense allowed, and three tickets meant automatic expulsion, the issue before us *would not be grammar, but rather tyranny.* Once a system like that is in place, it will not be long before subject-verb tickets are being issued for anything that an abusive officer happens to dislike.

And it is precisely here that we have gone off the rails. There are those who believe they are engaged in the work of racial reconciliation, but the effect of their labors is precisely the opposite. It is appropriate to call a Klansman a racist. It is appropriate to identify exercises in lowering the bar for blacks as racist. It is appropriate to say that certain jokes are now considered to be in bad taste. All that is fair game, each at the appropriate level.

But when apostles of reconciliation call you a despicable racist for simply saying that we ought to hear back from the grand jury first, notice what has happened. They are now saying that any defense of due process is to be identified out of hand as a defense of racism. If they call you vile names for asking if the crime actually happened— when you grant that the crime would be evil if it did in fact happen—they are attacking, not the hegemony of racism, but rather the rule of law.

To revile due process is to become, in principle, a defender of lynchings. When the controversy erupts, any caution against acting hastily is perversely taken as a defense of the alleged crime itself. A century ago, if a black man were accused of raping a white woman, and a mob were starting to form in order to fetch him from the county jail, and you were trying to formulate a speech to give from the steps of that jail in order to stop them, what would you say? You should say that a defense of due process is never a defense of any crime whatever, if such a crime happened.

But our first duty lies there—if it happened. And those who want to guard the processes we use to find out such things are not the enemies of the downtrodden. Quite the reverse. When the protections of law are gone, it will not be the rich and well-connected who suffer.

So as our college campuses spiral out of control, the loss of due process there amounts to the loss of everyone's liberty. It promises, in the not-too-distant future, to again plant trees with "strange fruit" on them. To go along with any level of this PC foolishness is like going on a bender in Bangkok and getting a tattoo from a guy whose English is not that strong.

CHAPTER 10

ALL LIES MATTER

Someone once observed, sagely, that it is not necessary to choose up sides in an ethnic war. The other side does that for you. Put another way, there are some things you can't opt out of. But considered from another angle, in the meantime there are certain things that Christians should strive to understand better than we currently do.

The July 2016 shootings, in Minneapolis, Baton Rouge, and then Dallas[1] set off a nationwide reaction that is the result of our identity politics come home to roost. There is a massive tendency to simply identify such incidents with race when there is actually far more going on.

The problem is not only that we identify with our tribes before Christ, but also that, in our confusion, we have

---

1. Philando Castile was killed by a police officer at a traffic stop on July 6, 2016. Alton Sterling was shot by Baton Rouge police on July 5, 2016. On July 17, Gavin Eugene Long shot six Baton Rouge police officers, killing three. Micah Xavier Johnson shot fourteen Dallas police officers, killing five, on July 7, 2016.

gotten our tribes all wrong. We are idolaters, which is bad enough, but then we have gone and gotten the name of the idol all wrong.

Andrew Breitbart once observed that politics is downstream from culture. I would add that culture is downstream from worship and faith. A right understanding of this explains why Christian conservatives have been so disappointed over the last few decades. We have been fighting in the right war, but have been fighting from the wrong end. We have been fighting politically, which is most necessary, but we have been fighting as though culture were irrelevant to this political battle, which is why we have been losing it.

NO CULTURAL CHANGE WITHOUT CULTURES CHANGING

The presenting characteristics of an ethnic group or tribe are largely a function of culture. The racist wants it to be that the presenting characteristics of an ethnic group, particularly the negative characteristics of a despised group, are genetic. These problems, or so the thinking goes, are just the way things *are*.

But this is not what the Bible teaches.

"One of themselves, even a prophet of their own, said, The Cretans are alway liars, evil beasts, slow bellies. This witness is true. Wherefore rebuke them sharply, that they may be sound in the faith" (Titus 1:12–13). There was a distinct Cretan culture, one which Epimenides observed, and which caused the apostle Paul to cite him favorably as he was equipping Titus for pastoral ministry in Crete. Note that a generalization is given, to the disadvantage of Cretans generally, which was (for Christians) true.

God thought what Paul said. Cretans, in marked distinction from other ethnic groups, were liars, animals, and slow bellies. But notice what Paul tells Titus to do about it. He says that he was to rebuke them sharply, *so that they might be sound in the faith.*

In other words, the call of Christian discipleship does not write off any ethnic group any more than it writes off sinful individuals. People can change, and, as a result, families, households, and tribes can change, which means that, over time, cultures can change. The power of the gospel transforms more than individuals.

In His last charge, Jesus said that we were to disciple the *ethnoi*, baptizing them and teaching them to obey Him in everything. Those are our marching orders. We are not given the option of saying that this particular tribe among the *ethnoi* is incorrigible. To the extent that we cling to our racism, *we* are trying to be incorrigible.

The mission assigned by Christ does not really have the modern nation-state in view. Depending on which one it is, the modern nation-state can have a heavy ethnic element, or over time it can become its own *ethnos.* But *ethnoi*, tribes, are primarily in view. And He did not say that we were to teach obedience to all the tribes except for the obvious loser tribes. We are to preach the good news of salvation to every creature, and to the tribes they were born into.

"And they sung a new song, saying, Thou art worthy to take the book, and to open the seals thereof: for thou wast slain, and hast redeemed us to God by thy blood out of every kindred, and tongue, and people, and nation; And hast made us unto our God kings and priests: and we shall reign on the earth" (Rev. 5:9–10).

Note bene: There are those who believe they are being insulting to blacks when they are actually insulting and taunting the power of the death of Jesus. Where some would see bigotry, I see something closer to blasphemy.

But Word-centered Christians need to labor to keep the *truth* of the gospel, and the *power* of the gospel, front and center in all of this. And why? Because all lies matter.

TRIBES, NOT RACES

One of the besetting sins of white liberals is their insistence on reducing their beloved identity politics to the most superficial level possible—to that of the epidermis, regardless of cultural affiliations and loyalties which run far closer to the bone. But the real driver of behavior is *culture*, and behind that is the relationship of that cultural tribe to God and His Word. What behaviors are common in that group, and, more to the point, what behaviors receive the social approval of that group generally?

But liberals just want to look at the skin. For example, liberals saw South Africa in black and white, instead of seeing three major black tribes (Zulu, Xhosa, and Sotho) and two major white ones (English and Dutch).

They see the white man conquering North America, taking it away from a group called "Native Americans." But the Native Americans were made up of numerous tribes, very different from one another, with different languages, cultures, and so on. They were often deadly enemies to one another. And anyone who cannot tell the difference between the Nez Perce and the Comanche really ought not to be contributing to the discussion. I, for one, would be fully in favor of the state of Idaho seizing federal lands in

Idaho, and returning a bunch of it to the Nez Perce, whom we did in fact rip off in a terrible way. But other tribes do not have my sympathy at all. Why? Because while tribes have an obvious genetic component, they are not defined by race, and they are not determined by it.

Tamerlane was racially distinct from the lands in the West that he invaded, but it would be a mistake to think he was conducting a war on "white people." That categorization does not really apply.

So once you have divided Americans neatly up into "white" and "black," you immediately have trouble explaining why someone who descended from people who arrived here in the 1920s from Lithuania owes anything to blacks whose ancestors were abused by Englishmen in the 1720s. If your grandparents fled Auschwitz and settled in Brooklyn, what do you owe blacks who had to deal with bigotry in Selma? Really? Skin color is all it takes?

In the centuries when millions of blacks were being enslaved and shipped from West Africa in the Middle Passage, the same thing was happening in reverse as Muslim raiders were capturing slaves from Europe as far north as Ireland. The very name *slave* comes from *Slav*, and as many as a million Europeans were captured and taken off into slavery—should we demand reparations from Libya now? And who are "we," exactly?

If you reduce everything to skin color, you are like someone whose library catalog system puts all the red books over here, and all the gray ones over there. But what do the books say? What are they *about*? Shouldn't we file them in accordance with what they are saying? *Red book! Red book! Hater!*

Superficial analysis also has a great deal of trouble explaining the difference in accomplishment between West Indian blacks in America and American blacks in America. In culture quite different, they both had slavery as part of their legacy. In culture they are quite different, but with differences that would make no difference at all to the bigot who is refusing to hire blacks. And yet, West Indian blacks excelled here. Why? Because culture is a far more powerful driver than liberals want to believe.

In short, white liberalism is profoundly racist. The fact that their racism is patronizing and declared to be well-meaning changes nothing. Everything for them reduces to skin color, and the omnicompetent oppressions of whitey. Thus, in a manner of speaking, they want Koreans and Chinese to "stick together." But somebody really ought to read a book sometime.

So culture trumps politics, but it also trumps pigmentation. Tribes are a cultural phenomenon, and not primarily a genetic, racial one. Culture has to do with shared language, expectations, sexual mores, values, and so on, and behind all of it, the God who is worshiped or not. If you are among those who assume that pigmentation settles culture, then you are a big part of our problem.

BLACK CRACKER CULTURE

If you insist on "zooming out" and evaluating black culture with "blackness" as the sole determining variable of the group you are studying, what you will find is manifest inferiority. You will find a dysfunctional mess—high levels of criminality, illegitimacy, substandard education, and other forms of destructive behavior. This was not created by the welfare state, but the welfare state has most certainly grievously exacerbated it—a welfare state that was the brain child of officious white people. As Paul would say, therefore rebuke *them* sharply ...

When you find, as you will, that black Americans have many more run-ins with the cops than do white citizens, you shouldn't put on a shocked face. Blacks are around 12 percent of the total American population, and make up around 35 percent of the prison population. You will have to give some account of this. If you are a liberal, you will blame white privilege, the legacy of slavery, etc. If you are a racist, you will blame the incorrigible nature of blacks. But if you are a Christian, you will blame the world, the flesh, and the devil, and you will undertake the task of "rebuking them sharply" so that they might be sound in the faith.

Those who minister among blacks ought not labor to have their rebukes line up with some sort of egalitarian cultural mythology. The sins rebuked should be the sins actually on display, the sins that are destroying the people. The different sins destroying other people in other places and in other ways are not relevant.

Now as Thomas Sowell has shown, this particular culture originally arose in the border lands between England and Scotland, in Ulster and the highlands. We are talking about cracker culture, the culture of poor whites in the American South. In many ways, this culture parallels the culture of poor blacks in the South, and there has historically been a great deal of traffic between the two. Regardless, it is destructive. Sexual promiscuity and violence are not the key elements in building a civilization, whether you are white or black.

But if you zoom in and examine particuiar black sub-cultures, you will find *more than one*. You will quickly discover that black *genetics* have nothing whatever to do with lack of accomplishment. The culprit is disobedient *culture*, which is the result of the collective choices of individuals over generations.

NOW TO SOME POLICING PARTICULARS

As more details emerged from the July 2016 shooting incidents, the more it became obvious that trial by Facebook is not something we really ought to be striving for. This includes judgments passed on cops and civilians both.

The reason we should want to have an honest judicial system is so that disinterested investigators can methodically get all the facts, find out the back story, interview all the witnesses, and make a determination. This would result in an indictment or not, and afterward a trial if needed. Sometimes the determination must be made in the field, as was the case with the Dallas sniper. It is easier to find out what is going on when someone tells the world what he is doing and why. But other times the investigation is going to take the weeks and months following, where the suspect denies doing what we think he might have done. This is not the same thing as passing judgment in the hours following the incident on Twitter.

But here is our dilemma. When our official establishment has disgraced itself time and again through various shenanigans and cover-ups, it is harder for those who want a judicious and impartial inquiry to be able to call for one, as I want to be able to do.

Here's an example within recent memory. James Comey of the FBI achieved something of a milestone when he was, as lead investigator, placed under oath in order to reveal that the target of an investigation had not been placed under oath. His testimony was recorded, and Hillary's testimony was not recorded.

One of the reasons why a justice system has to be manifestly uncorrupted is that people will not stop rioting in the streets in order to let a corrupt system handle their grievances. When the establishment has lost the respect of respectable people, they have lost pretty much everything. And everyone else lost something crucial, too.

In the meantime, I object to the militarization of our police. I object to the inane nanny-state laws that they are called upon to enforce. I object to the politicization of the judicial system, using it as a weapon on merely political foes. I object to the war on drugs. I object to corrupt cops who disable their bodycams prior to mischief. But most of all, I object to partisans who care more for the interests of their tribe (whether a long-standing tribe or in a developing *ad hoc* tribe) than in the requirements of biblical justice.

I can't be on the side of the Oregon ranch protesters over against the authorities because of the color of the protesters, and then be on the side of the authorities when they pull over someone for driving while black. I am a Christian *first*, and that means the principles of biblical justice first, and that means that in any given situation, a different tribe might need to be rebuked sharply.

In short, Eric Garner and Michael Brown were not in the same category at all, and we need a judicial system capable of telling the difference. If someone's analysis of the situation consists of looking at the color of the fabric on the ones who did the killing, and the Ancestry.com sheet of the one who was killed, then that person really ought to be banned from jury duty for life.

If you want to read up on some of these things, here are just a couple recommendations. I've already mentioned *Life at the Bottom* by Theodore Dalrymple for evidence that all the inner city pathologies that we see among black people here in America can be readily manifested by white people just as well. Thomas Sowell has also addressed this problem in very trenchant detail in his essay *Black Rednecks and White Liberals*, found in a book with the same name.[2] If you want to know my take on race relations in America, I am pretty much where Sowell is.

NOT DIFFERENT TRUTHS, JUST DIFFERENT TRIBES AND TEAMS

Another trial by Twitter, and another example of drawing tribal lines in the wrong places, took place after the May 14, 2022, shooting at a Buffalo, N.Y., supermarket, where ten black people were killed and three others injured.

It happened on this wise. Author Jackie Hill Perry tweeted this:

> Say what ya want about Farrakhan (because there's a whole lot to say) but this right here is facts. #BuffaloMassacre #ReplacementTheory[3]

And this was accompanied by a clip of Louis Farrakhan dispensing what some people in these misbegotten days

2. *Black Rednecks and White Liberals* (San Francisco: Encounter Books, 2006).
3. Jackie Hill Perry (@JackieHillPerry). Twitter, May 22, 2022, 7:36 a.m. (account deleted).

might want to regard as wisdom. I wouldn't know; I didn't watch it.

To which Phil Johnson, executive director *Grace to You*, of responded,

> Folks, when someone who is perpetually platformed by Big Eva starts pointing people to Louis Farrakhan as a source of factual & spiritual insight, that's all the proof you need that Big Eva & Woke dogma have passed their use-by date.[4]

To which Anthony Bradley responded,

> @JackieHillPerry does not need to apologize for this LF clip because what he said in this particular clip is true. Truth is truth.[5]

To which *I* responded ...

As we are now speaking of truth being the truth, let us dig in to find a bit of truth that we might find useful in these troubled times of ours. If the principle articulated by Bradley here is a sound one, then we should be able to apply it in disparate situations, and come away satisfied that we have tested the rule and found it to be straight line true.

So Jackie Hill Perry "does not need to apologize" for having quoted a controversial figure because, as far as the words within the quotation went, they were true. If Farrakhan

---

4. Phil Johnson (@Phil_Johnson_). Twitter, May 22, 2022, 4:26 p.m. https://twitter.com/Phil_Johnson_/status/1528517801014464513.
5. Anthony B. Bradley (@drantbradley). Twitter, on or about May 22, 2022 (tweet no longer available).

believes other things that are either loopy or full of bile, we may discount all of that because none of it was included in the quote in question. Furthermore, a defender of Jackie Hill Perry could even say that she went so far as to put some daylight between her and the fruitier emanations from Monsieur Farrakhan (i.e., "because there's a whole lot to say . . .").

Now even granting this principle, which for the sake of argument we are now doing, one sees that the principle likely has some natural limits. Say that Adolph Hitler delivered himself of the view that two and two equals four, and that the sun invariably rises in the east. If you were arguing these points in an academic paper, you might want to pick a less distracting source to buttress your argument, and this seems really understandable. So let us limit our application of this principle to situations less extreme than those created by genocidal maniacs doing simple math, or watching the sun rise.

So then, granting these natural limits, which we all understand, we now have our rule. Shall we apply it equitably? Shall we bring in equal weights and measures, not to mention a mixed metaphor, and see how Anthony Bradley likes them apples?

Suppose somebody taken at random, a Douglas Wilson, say, quoted one R.L. Dabney favorably on an issue like secular education. The quotation was accurate and true as far as it went, meaning that everything between the quotation marks was right on the money.

> Christians must prepare themselves then, for the following results: All prayers, catechisms, and Bibles will ultimately be driven out of the schools . . . . Humanity always

finds out, sooner or later, that it cannot get on without a religion, and it will take a false one in preference to none.[6]

Now I suspect that Anthony Bradley would rather be dead in a ditch than go along with this. He would say that Dabney, an unreconstructed Confederate, was a disgrace to evangelical and Reformed theology, no better than a Nazi, and that he should under no circumstances be platformed in any way by anybody today, even when he was saying something true. Actually, *especially* when he was saying something true, because impressionable types might read him on the true stuff and think that this helps to validate anything else he might have been saying, and so they proceed from accepting what he said about the impossibility of secular education to an acceptance of what he said in his *Systematic Theology* about the innate inferiority of redheads. Which he did in fact say. As Jackie Hill Perry might say, if she were putting daylight between herself and Dabney, and if she were here, "there's a whole lot to say."

Okay, so now we have ourselves a new rule, a little different than the earlier one. Actually, it is the opposite of the earlier one. *Now* a person who says true things in one setting and outrageous things in another setting must not be listened to at all. To affirm such a person at any one point is the same thing as affirming whatever they might hold about anything else, and to quote them favorably at any one point entails one (does it not?) in all their perfidy. By this means, Anthony Bradley dispenses of me and my Dabney quotes, and good riddance says he, but doesn't

6. R.L. Dabney, *On Secular Education* (Moscow, ID: Canon Press, 1996), 29.

this mean that Jackie Hill Perry now needs to apologize for commending anything that came out of the mouth of that Farrakhan guy?

Sauce for the goose, as Heidegger the Nazi once put it.

But something else is going on actually. Anthony Bradley said that truth is truth. What he should have said was "tribes are tribes." What he should have said is "teams are teams." Whenever partisan feeling runs high, and your team is on the three-yard-line late in the fourth quarter, and you score, but then one of the refs makes a call that pulls the touchdown back, and everybody is yelling, the sentiments about the accuracy of that call is likely to be seriously divided. Different parts of the stadium see it differently. And a yelling fan might say something like "truth is truth," just like Anthony Bradley did, but he is actually yelling the way he is because teams are teams.

The thing that is complicated in our day is that many of the fans in the evangelical bleachers are in the process of switching teams, switching allegiances. And so the bad call happened right when they had one fan jersey off and the other one halfway on. Now what? They can't really appeal to team spirit *simpliciter* because that part is all confused now. And so they appeal to "the truth," as though anybody is clear about what that is anymore.

So these are confusing times. Times of uncertainty. Few things are stable anymore. But despite all this, I do think that we can still say one thing with real confidence. If Jackie Hill Perry had quoted Douglas Wilson instead of Louis Farrakhan, she would have already had to apologize by now. Repeatedly. And at Anthony Bradley's insistence.

I speak the truth here and, as we all know, truth is truth.

CHAPTER 11

WHAT IS THE MATTER WITH BLACK LIVES MATTER?

Taken at face value, the phrase *black lives matter* is a phrase that no sensible person could differ with. Of course they do. Also taken at face value, the rejoinder *all lives matter* is equally true. Of course *they* do.

The reason for the back and forth, then, has nothing to do with the meaning of the phrases as they might be ascertained from the dictionary, or from a normal person interested in social stability. Rather, we need to be attuned to the *political* meanings of the phrases, and in order to determine that we have to look at current usage. Put another way, black lives matter would be a wonderful sentiment if we found it in a personal letter of William Wilberforce to his mother. In the mouth of a black agitator calling for the murder of cops, it is an abuse of language, an instance of outrageous and hateful slang. When he says "black lives matter," it would be better to reply instantly, "No, *in the sense you are intending*, no, they don't."

FRANKFURT AGITPROP

Black lives matter is agitprop right out of the Frankfurt school, and they are doing a bang-up job with it, incidentally, about which more in a minute.

And it probably goes without saying that guilt-ridden white liberals love the phrase for reasons related to David Stove's trenchant phrase—he refers to whites who "having renounced the pleasures of power...discover the pleasures of guilt."[1] This goes double for the evangelical racial healers, who—in possession of the Holy Spirit—do for our race relations what Benny Hinn does for rheumatoid arthritis.

I saw one cute cartoon—cute in the sense of *arch*—that showed a house burning down, with the firemen hosing down the house next to it because, as they put it, "all houses matter." But of course this misconstrues the scene entirely. It ought to show firemen hosing down the house on fire, with cops arresting the arsonists, who were hiding in the house next door. The fact that the arsonists were shouting noble phrases on the way to the patrol car should not make us ignore the fact that they were the ones busy with the gas cans earlier.

CHRISTIAN AND COLOR BLIND

Sin, including racial sin, can only be committed in the *present*. We can and should seek to deal with downstream

1. David Stove, *Against the Idols of the Age* (New York: Routledge, 2017), 139.

ramifications of sin from the past—restitution, reconciliation, and so on—but we can never address the impact of
sin from the past by giving way to worse sin now. If you
are wanting to fix the scars from hatred past, hatred present is never the way.

Now, consider:

1. X shoots and kills Y. He claims that he did not intend
to do it. It was an accident. There are good reasons
to suspect that it might not have been an accident.

2. X shoots and kills Y. He claims that he did it inten-
tionally, and that all who look like Y should die in
a similar way.

In the first instance, you reserve judgment and arrange
for an investigation and trial. In the second, you do what
they did in Dallas. You should pursue this *whether or not* X
and Y are all white, all black, or some of each.

For anyone who loves Christ, that color part shouldn't
matter. "You shall not be partial in judgment. You shall hear
the small and the great alike. You shall not be intimidated by
anyone, for the judgment is God's" (Deut. 1:17, ESV).

Do we really need to know the color of X and Y in these
scenarios in order to determine what we think about them?
If you do not know how you would apply a moral judgment to such situations before knowing the color of X and
the color of Y, then—I am speaking frankly here—you are
in high rebellion against the Word of God. The Golden
Rule is neither black nor white. The Golden Rule is just the
color it is supposed to be.

ONE-WAY WAR

What the Black Lives Matter agitators are wanting is the lopsided circumstance of a one-way war. In a war, you are in lethal combat with a group, and if it is on a large enough scale you may find yourself having to fight (and perhaps kill) adversaries who were as decent as the slain Dallas cops were. That could happen, and it could happen in a just war. It could happen in either direction or in both, and that is part of what makes wars so terrible.

In police action, the desire is to take a criminal as a prisoner alive wherever possible. Having been apprehended, he is then to be given the presumption of innocence and a fair trial. In police work, you are dealing with individuals *as individuals*. Sometimes this is very difficult (as in a riot), but it is always the *desideratum*. When riot conditions become normal, what you actually have is *de facto* civil war.

Now what the incendiary rhetoric of Black Lives Matter wants is the rules of warfare in one direction and minimal police action in the other. And the answer is that such a thing is impossible. Being impossible, it may be tentatively ranked among those things that are not going to happen. They are not trying to make that impossibility happen. They are trying to make *chaos* happen so that they can be in a position to make *something else* happen. That something else is the revolution. All I can tell you, brother, is you have to wait.

I mentioned the Frankfurt School of Stage Four Critical Theory fame. In this view, those who belong to the oppressed classes cannot, by definition, be guilty of anything. Achieving membership in such a class is therefore quite a privilege. If you are black, you can't be a racist, for example. Correction, if you are the right kind of oppressed black you can't be a racist. Clarence Thomas can be racist because he has been ejected from the oppressed class for his misbehavior, which was, upon examination, thinking for himself.

ALWAYS BACK TO GOSPEL

Critical Theory is therefore a social theory that counterfeits the great gospel truth of justification. Aping the apostle, and trying to steal glory from the gospel of grace, the Black Lives Matter movement says to the most hateful and malicious people ... *no condemnation.*

But the words ring hollow because they are spoken by liars. Their message is not based on the substitutionary death of Jesus Christ. A preacher of the gospel can say *no condemnation,* but no one else can. If a preacher of the gospel undertakes to deliver this message, he must preach it *to every creature.* He must do it in the spirit of the words of the Sunday School song I learned when I was a kid—preach to red and yellow, black and white. Does that sound corny? Too bad.

This planet really is screwed up, and we do need preachers of the gospel declaring this message. But the no condemnation is offered indiscriminately to all—Jew and Greek, black and white, male and female, slave or free. It is offered because of the cross of Christ, and on that basis alone.

Black Lives Matter denies this gospel, and anyone who carries water for them is thinking about doing the same.

BLACK LYNCH MOBS

The September 2016 shootings of two black men—Terence Crutcher in Tulsa and Keith Scott in Charlotte—set off another round of racial turmoil, not to mention another round of Orwellian news and news analysis.

Let us revisit some basic definitions. *Protesters* are those who assemble peaceably to register their views on something, or their insistence that something be done. *Violent protesters* are those who clash physically with the police who were guarding their protest. *Rioters* are those who indiscriminately attack the innocent for the sake of their ostensible cause. I use the word *ostensible* because a distinction needs to be made between the cause of racial justice and harmony on the one hand, and the cause of not having a big enough flat screen on the other.

Because Black Lives Matter is an organization that already knows what it thinks about the *next* incident where a black man is killed by cops, the details and facts surrounding that next incident clearly don't matter, just as the details about *this* one don't matter. Now this means that the rule of law doesn't matter to them. And because the rule of law is one of the hallmarks of any civilized society, the BLM are revealing themselves to be nothing more than Black Lynch Mobs.

If you compare the Tulsa shooting with the Charlotte shooting, there appeared to be much more of a cause for legitimate complaint in Tulsa, where protests occurred, than in Charlotte, where rioting did. In Tulsa, there certainly appeared to be enough evidence to *indict* the white officer who shot Terence Crutcher. If she indeed had shot him "just in case," then she should have received appropriate legal consequences. The aerial footage of that incident looked bad—but even with that said, *there still had to be a trial* where she had every reasonable opportunity to defend herself. But in Charlotte, where an armed black man was shot by a black officer, representing a department with a black police chief—naturally setting off a series of riots against whitey—the situation was quite different.

"Last night in City X, a _____ police officer stopped a _____ motorist in a routine traffic stop. The _____ officer apparently gave a command and stepped back toward the rear of the car. Aerial footage showed the motorist emerging from his vehicle with his hands in the air, but moments later he was on the ground, having been shot by the officer seven times."

Again, if you are the kind of person who needs to know the colors that fill in those blanks before knowing what you think of this, then you are the kind of person who ought to do us all a favor by using every trick possible to get out of jury duty.

Now let us say, for the sake of discussion, that the shooting of Keith Lamont Scott in Charlotte was simple murder by the cops. Let's make the murdering cop white, and let us make the motivation bigotry *simpliciter*, and let us say that the Charlotte police department is riddled with seething racial hatred. If the response is to riot, targeting people who had nothing whatever to do with the original offense, then you have successfully accomplished what so many before you have accomplished: *You have become a differently tinted version of your enemy.* Your skin is a different color, but your hearts are the same color.

I don't like Kant much, but I do like his formulation of the Golden Rule—so behave that you would be willing for your behavior to become a universal law. If a legitimate response to a white murder of a black man is to select a random white bystander and kill him, then a legitimate response to a black murderer would be the photo negative of that. And if you want to live in a society governed by rules like *that*, the kind of "rules" that BLM foments, then you are clearly much fonder of adrenaline than I am.

At this point in the discussion—when the progressive defense of indefensible lawlessness becomes obvious—they usually want to turn the discussion to "root causes," "systemic racism," and so on. We have to address the *root* causes of racial unrest, they say. Okay, we can talk about that, but you are not going to successfully address the root causes until you are willing to outlaw all municipal governance by black Democrats.

ON DIVORCING THE DEMOCRATS

And what do I mean by that? Let us begin by granting that American blacks are the battered spouse in an abusive relationship. There are aspects to the analogy that are very easy to see—because the bruises are so readily identifiable. The abuse is very real. But because it is an analogy that compares groups containing millions of people with a marriage containing two people, there *are* ways that the analogy can go astray. In fact, that difficulty is one of the chief tools that the real abuser uses to perpetuate his abuse.

Who then is the abusive spouse? Is it white America? Is it the more nebulous culprit that is being called white privilege? Is it the history of race-based slavery? Is it something that Calhoun said? Or is the problem (much) closer to home?

Remember, one of the marked features of battered wife syndrome is the *learned helplessness*—as one article put it, she has "psychological paralysis—where the victim becomes so depressed, defeated, and passive that she believes she is incapable of leaving the abusive situation." Not only so, but between episodes, the battered wife learns to make excuses for the abuser, for remaining in the relationship with him. He promised to be better. She might even learn to attack anyone who suggests that she leave, as though a genuine offer of outside help were the problem.

As we look around our cultural landscape, thinking in terms of this analogy, is there any group that American blacks are *married to,* and which is a group that does appalling things to them in return? The answer really is plain—the abusive spouse in this comparison is the Democratic Party. Remember that an abusive spouse is one who *does* things; he has to have policies and *actions* that have terrible consequences. The abuse is the kind that leaves a bruise.

Think about it for a moment. Make a list of cities that the Democratic Party has had *complete control of* for a generation or more—Detroit, Baltimore, Chicago, say. Are these places paradises that blacks stream to because the opportunities are so wonderful? Right—they are nothing of the kind. They look like downtown Beirut after the most recent outrage. They are tangled nests of corruption, conflict and crime.

Which party adopted welfare policies that created economic incentives for massive illegitimacy, and then was astonished at the subsequent wave of illegitimacy? Which party imposed the abortion carnage on our nation, resulting in a grotesquely disproportionate number of black children being executed? Which party is run by economic nincompoops who never met a job-creator that they didn't want to fine heavily until he fled the state, taking his jobs with him? Which party promotes race-hustling quislings to positions of high honor? Which party honors rap artists who *celebrate* deeply destructive patterns of human behavior? Which party attacks any attempts to do basic budgetary math as though *that* were deeply and profoundly racist?

And if you don't want to follow what might appear at first glance to be arcane arguments, just content yourself with looking at the results. Whenever socialism—the singular mania of the Democrats—is imposed anywhere, it is the death of that place. It has been imposed on black America, and it was imposed on black America by the Democrats. The results have been an unmitigated disaster. The ones who should be held responsible should be the ones who did it. I have no objection to black leaders calling abuse. It is long past time for them to do so. But they ought to call abuse on *the one who is actually hitting them.* Your next-door neighbor has been urging you to leave for some time now, and I think this would be a good time to stop calling *her* the racist.

So in using the abused wife metaphor—which I think is most necessary—it is also necessary to ask and answer the most basic questions. The first one is this: "Is this an abusive relationship?" The answer is plainly *yes.* But the second question is equally critical: "Who are you *married* to?" When you finally get the divorce, what names will be on that paper?

ATHEISM AND MEANINGLESS BLACK LIVES

Whence cometh this abusive behavior? A lot of cyber ink has been spilled when it comes to responses and critiques of the Black Lives Matter movement. But it has to be said that many of these critiques, however good, have merely plucked leaves or branches off the tree. What I would like to do in this space is borrow a 28-inch Husqvarna chain saw from John the Baptist and have him show me how to lay something like that at the root of the tree.

Much of the tussling has been because normal people want to say something sweet and reasonable, like "*all* lives matter," and they point out that it follows necessarily that black lives would also matter, being a subset of all lives as they are. The response to this claim is that white supremacists are plenty clever enough to nip in and get control of any kind of All Lives control panel, and do so in such a way as to perpetuate the inequities between whites and blacks, which means that, at the end of the day All Lives Matter would turn into some version of All Lives Matter, but Some Don't Matter as Much. Thus, to say anything like this is to betray that you don't know what the Black Lives Matter people are talking about, not even a little bit.

And, I must say, if we all agreed that Jesus rose from the dead, they might have a point in there worth considering and discussing. But we don't share any kind of transcendental commitments, which means that all these pretended advocates of justice have simply surrendered the field. We still might dispute with one another, but the dispute doesn't signify. It just means that we are dogs yapping at each other endlessly at midnight.

I say this because the founders of Black Lives Matter were basically atheistic Marxists, which means that their actual position necessarily reduces to No Lives Matter. By *atheism* here, I mean both atheism proper and functional atheism—where there may be an appeal to tiny gods that can fit on a tribal shelf. These are arbitrary gods with no transcendent authority and, ultimately, the ramifications will be the same. We need to look at them straight on.

One of those ramifications is a helpful explanation of the irrational black rage we see exploding all around us. All of it is just naked envy of the successes of what they call white supremacy, but I am getting a little ahead of myself. Someone needs to tell me to cool my baby jets.

PHARISAICAL ATHEISM

One of the things I have noticed in my interactions with atheists is the fact that they are very good at getting themselves into a fever pitch of moral indignation. It is one of their signature moves. Hitchens used to do it, Dawkins does it, and Harris does it. They banish any and all possible grounds for any kind of moral evaluation at all, and then they wheel on you, jowls quivering and anger in their eyes, like a Victorian archbishop who just found a couple of painted ladies in the choir loft.

If there is no God, then we are all just inchoate chemical assemblages and random neuron firings, and all of our moral indignation over this travesty or that outrage are on exactly the same level as what happens when you pour vinegar into baking soda. Something awful happens, and there you are, foaming away at it, and above you . . . only sky. So change that "something awful" into "something that apparently displeased the baking soda."

Let me make the point even plainer. If there is no God, then—as Dostoevsky noted—all is permitted. And if all is permitted, then that means that white supremacy is permitted, lynching uppity blacks is permitted, separate drinking fountains are just fine, the Tuskegee syphilis experiments were the way to go, more people than Dave Chappelle can use the N-word with impunity (that word being *November*), and so on. There will be no judgment, there will be no reckoning, there will be no last assizes.

And if people who do not believe in God are in the middle of the mob, fomenting rage, you can rest assured that you are dealing, not with a social justice advocate, but rather with an intricate and very clever hustle.

In our previous Christian consensus, the oppression mattered, and so the hustle works this way. The hustle wants to squeeze every possible concession out of that waning Christian consensus, as long as it lasts, and then to move on to the next lucrative opportunity. Socialist paradises don't offer too many of those, and so the ideal would be to find another host body with lots of money and a reservoir of guilt. The problem they will confront is that when America is gone, the tapeworm will lament having killed the last fat guy. And you haven't seen forlorn sorrow until you see a tapeworm who wouldn't think ahead.

NOT ONLY SO

Not only so, but this means more than saying that living atheists have a right to embrace ethical nihilism if they so desire. It also means that dead atheists in generations past had the right to live that way back in the day. YOLO, man. And it means that the slave trader back then, cracking the whip, and the ardent abolitionist back then, trying hard to outlaw the slave trade, are now, *both of them*, a set of bleached bones, the color of the moon. None of it matters, and nobody cares. In fact, the abolitionist had his statue vandalized with red paint and pulled over first.

And do you know what that means? It means that the architects of white supremacy, who built all this evil infrastructure around us, did not actually do anything evil—for there is no such thing, remember?—but they did successfully do what benefited them and their tribe. And this means that all those white oppressors, now dead and gone, *got away with it.*

Nathan Bedford Forrest, founder of the Klan, got clean away with it.

> If after the manner of men I have fought with beasts at
> Ephesus, what advantageth it me, if the dead rise not?
> let us eat and drink; for to morrow we die. (1 Cor. 15:32)

If the dead are not raised, if there is no "savior religion," then Ibram X. Kendi can do whatever he wants. But then again, so could the white supremacists of yore, and so could Stalin, and so could Pol Pot, and so can Donald Trump and Jerry Seinfeld and Ammon Bundy and Kyle Rittenhouse and Ted Cruz and anyone else you manage to recruit for this meaningless protoplasm parade of yours.

KNOW WHAT ELSE?

Know what else it means? It means that because God cannot bring justice to these malefactors, since He doesn't exist and they are all dead, it also follows that Ibram X. Kendi can't bring any kind of justice to them either. They are completely out of his reach. They pulled off the perfect crime. They were white, and then decided to go off to build the mechanisms of white supremacy, which have functioned smoothly on their behalf for centuries. They gathered their personal fortunes from the sale of Haitian cane sugar, they sat on the veranda of their plantation houses with their wives and three children, they went back to the slave cabins to beget little mulatto sons and daughters as the whim took them, and they generally swanked around as sweet as all dammit.

Who may condemn this kind of thing? Certainly not any atheists. But that, of course, is only if we require the atheists to be consistent, which, given atheism, they have no obligation to be.

So the best that Kendi can do is go to a Benjamin Moore outlet, get a color swatch, and then writhe and spit at people who kind of match the tint of the oppressors. And yet frustration is not justice. It might explain why a man dealing with an irascible boss comes home and kicks the dog, but kicking the dog is just a proxy sort of thing. And everybody in the house knows it . . . except for the dog.

The dog is the kind of creature who will accept all the blame. He knows that he is the problem. The argument seems compelling to him, because the color swatch *did* match up in a way that was almost uncanny. These people—pasty patsies, let us call them—are your NPR listeners, your evangelical pastors with ripped jeans and a Biden sticker on their guitar case, and your suburban white women who read liberation theology for their wine and cheese book groups.

WHATEVER HE WANTS

So if Ibram X. Kendi can do whatever he wants, which appears to be what he is in fact doing, I would tell him, given his premises, that he needs to cultivate more of a love-hate thing with the white supremacists of long ago. They successfully did what he is attempting to do. Why not take notes? Why not acknowledge your indebtedness? The guilt trip is not going to work very much longer, and so it will be time to pivot pretty soon.

But this is only a good idea if Christ did not rise from the dead. But Christ did in fact rise from the dead, which means that there is a savior religion with true authority.

BLACK HEARTS MATTER

Black Lives Matter is the mantra of an ideological collective. Individual black lives do not matter to them, not even a little bit. A black voice matters, in this scheme, only if it is serving as an avatar of that collective. And that collective is nothing more than a commie construct. Dismembered black children, scraped out of black wombs, do not advance the cause of the collective, and so *they* don't matter. Dissenting black conservative voices do not serve the collective, and so they are dismissed as the black face of white supremacy. The Christian faith, which served as an incredible solace to the black church in its time of exile, is contemptuously set aside as one of the chains. And it was a chain that did, in fact, bind the collective, but it did that by setting black Christians free.

The only place where individual black lives matter is in Christ. And, as it turns out, that is the only place where white lives can matter also. Christ is the only one in whom *anything* matters. In Christ, all things hold together, and apart from Him nothing holds together (Col. 1:17–18).

But Christ does not simply grant meaning to black individuals as such, or to white individuals as such. He grants everything that fallen men and women need— He gives forgiveness, restoration, holiness, and glory to black sinners and to white sinners. Regardless of the color of our skin, we all share the same color of sin. You can describe those sins as scarlet, or you can describe them as black, or as crimson, or as any other color that will upset somebody, but Christ will make them as white as snow, as white as wool.

And one of the things that will happen when Christ sets you free is that you will be able to handle color metaphors like a grown-up.

> Come now, and let us reason together, saith the Lord: Though your sins be as scarlet, they shall be as white as snow; Though they be red like crimson, they shall be as wool. (Isa. 1:18)

One of the games that sinners like to play is the game of grading on a curve. "Yes, I may have sinned, but at least I am not as bad as . . ." But God does not grade on a curve. He puts Capernaum into the same absolute scales of justice that He uses for Sodom, and Tyre, and Sidon. So if any of your children have ever been sold by Planned Parenthood, in lucrative pieces, then the slave traders of old Charleston will rise up and condemn you at the last day.

CHAPTER 12

SEVEN PRINCIPLES FOR NAVIGATING TIMES OF RACIAL ANIMOSITY

have seen Jon Gabriel's tweet many times, and, unfortunately, this is because there have been numerous occasions in the last few years where the snark fits like a glove: "My favorite part about the Obama era is all the racial healing."[1] I am old enough to remember 1967, and I am starting to feel the same foreboding crackle in the air. Hope I am wrong, but if not here are some thoughts that I trust may be helpful.

1. Avoid euphemisms for sin. In racial or ethnic conflicts, the sin is almost always found either in malice or in vainglory. Malice, or animosity, contradicts the Lord's requirement to love your enemies (Matt. 5:44), and vainglory tries to boast in real (or imagined) gifts as though

---

1. Jon Gabriel (@exjon), Twitter, November 24, 2014. Tweet no longer available.

the credit for having them was your own (1 Cor. 4:7). The charge of "racism" is far too general, and provides too much wiggle room for rationalization for those disposed to resist the charge. That, and it also makes a conceited secular culture the arbiter of "forgiveness" — far too much wiggle room for those who want to make the accusation. We have gotten to the ludicrous point where those who are "guilty" of microracism are treated as though they owned a fleet of slave ships.

So for a Christian, if it is sinful, then it is either animosity or arrogant pride. Sin is always against God and His Word. Sin has political consequences, but avoid putting politics in charge of the definition of sin.

2. Keep a level head, which means you don't measure justice by whatever you might think is good for your faction. Wherever God has placed you in a time of tension, there will be people in your "tribe" who behave wickedly. A level-headed person knows and understands this. David knew that Joab was on his side in Israel's civil conflict, and he also knew that Joab was a godless man.

3. Realize that there are people in the "other" tribe who are laboring to keep a level head as well. Don't make *their* job more difficult. Not only did David know that Joab was a scoundrel, he knew that Abner was noble. You cannot avoid conflict with fools, but never willingly burn your bridges with those who are not fools, *especially* if they are an adversary or even an enemy. Distinguish between irrational partisans of a position, and those who happen to hold convictions other than yours. In the political-racial-economic mess that we call race relations, make distinctions on the other side.

4. Don't use words like "dialogue" or "conversation" when what you have planned is a lecture. Cultivating this demeanor is a great help in avoiding a downward spiral into outbursts of anger. "Wherefore, my beloved brethren, let every man be swift to hear, slow to speak, slow to wrath" (James 1:19). Christians should be in the forefront of demonstrating how tense race relationships should go. We have all the same ingredients for tension as the world does, but one of the central accomplishments of justification by faith alone is the authority to tear down *every* middle wall of partition. In the body of Christ, everyone should be quick to listen. Everyone is to be slow to speak. Everyone must be slow to anger. In a Christian conversation, *everyone talks, and everyone tries to listen.*

5. Follow the money. But "follow the money" does not mean making room for the kind of envy and jealousy that pave the way for economic illiteracy. Racial unrest frequently follows economic troubles. Anyone familiar with the history of the world knows that different ethnic groups more easily come into conflict during times of scarcity and heightened competition for jobs. There are times when people feel that they cannot *afford* to lay down their hatred and suspicion. The Obama economy is just such a time. People still should turn away from hatred and suspicion, but in the meantime Christians should labor for a genuinely free market as a way of imitating the Father's willingness to "lead us not into temptation."

6. Do not confound rhetoric with accomplishments. In the Bible, hatred is defined by action, by behavior, and not by intentions. A man who refuses to discipline his son hates his son (Prov. 13:24), even if his negligence is for

sentimental reasons. As measured by *actions and their actual consequences*, people who support Planned Parenthood and their "Little Auschwitz Clinics" hate black people. Everyone who supports a $15 minimum wage hates black people. Those who do not want to abolish the government school system in the inner cities hate black people. Feel good gestures are no substitute for loving people in deed and truth. "If a brother or sister be naked, and destitute of daily food, suppose one of you say unto them, Depart in peace, be ye warmed and filled; have I not engaged in hashtag activism on thy behalf? Notwithstanding if ye give them not those things which are needful to the body; what doth it profit?" (Jas. 2:15–16).

But if you *were* to engage in hashtag activism, it ought to make some kind of moral and economic sense:

Defund Planned Parenthood. #BlackLivesMatter

Abolish the public school system. #BlackLivesMatter

Stop destroying black jobs—abolish minimum wage laws. #BlackLivesMatter

Abandon the draconian war on drugs. #BlackLivesMatter

Set up Jack Kemp's enterprise zones. #BlackLivesMatter

7. The tangled knot of sin in this world was a Gordian knot of epic proportions. Ethnic enmity has been standard operating procedure for millennia. Over the course of human history, slavery has been a very common affliction for

men and women of every color. Hatreds run deep, and if you run the animosity back far enough, everybody has a point. Everybody has a story. And outside of Christ, everyone renders universal by induction, and does so in a way that flatters their hatreds, and strokes their vainglory.

What this means is that *recriminations will fix nothing.* Apart from the cross of Christ, nothing is forgivable because all of it is inexcusable. But in Christ, the inexcusable can be forgiven. The gospel message requires all of us—red and yellow, black and white—to confess that our attitudes toward others have been inexcusable. They are not, however, thanks to God, unforgivable.

And 8. Get an education in the history of how we got here.

One last comment, lest anyone think that I believe the things outlined above do not apply to me or to my people. They most certainly do, all of them. At Christ Church, we confess our sins every week. In our liturgy, we first confess the sins of our nation, doing so as Christians on behalf of our countrymen. We do not exclude the sins described above. We then confess the sins of the church and the complicity of the church in the sins of the culture. We follow that up with a time of silent confession of our own sins as individuals.

When we confess the sins of our nation, we do not heal the wound lightly. Our confessions include some appalling behavior, and we know that if God were to destroy the United States for our sins, including our racial sins, there would be no injustice done.

But thanks be to God . . . when Christ died on the cross He made one new man out of all the old men. When we pray, we are asking for mercy, and not for justice.

CHAPTER 13

BRICKS MADE
OUT OF FOG

I would like to try to make a very simple point, but one which could be misconstrued in a thousand different ways. I would ask my friends not to do so, my enemies not to do so too violently, and for the vast horde wavering between friendship and hostility to read the whole thing before deciding anything rash.

REPENTANCE AND MISDIRECTION

In the summer of 2016, two denominations took a strong stand, or so they thought, against racism and the sins of the Old South. The Southern Baptist Convention (SBC) voted to "call our brothers and sisters in Christ to discontinue the display of the Confederate battle flag as a sign of solidarity of the whole Body of Christ, including our African-American brothers and sisters . . ."[1] And the Presbyterian Church in America (PCA) "overwhelmingly approved one overture confessing past and present sins of racism, and another to establish a study committee on racial reconciliation."[2]

At the same General Assembly, the PCA also decided to study the question of women in church office. If I had the camera on my computer turned on, you could catch a glimpse of my shocked face. If you have a cottage on the beach, the breezes blow in from off the bay. If you are in the PCA, the breezes blow in from Manhattan. Perhaps the problem, ye Presbyterians, is that you try to address problems like this with study committees. What a *white* thing to do.

NOW I SHOULDN'T HAVE TO SAY THIS . . .

Before getting to my point, which I do intend to make, I must repeat what I've already repeatedly said in this book: There really is such a thing as racial sin, whether it is racial vainglory or racial animosity. Sin is always sin, and God always hates it. Racism as defined by God is wickedness. Those who make a pet idol out of their skin tone, or who revile others because of their skin tone are the kind of people who go to Hell. They will not inherit the kingdom (1 Cor. 6:9–10). Racism, understood biblically, is no bagatelle.

So anyone who wants to represent what follows as an attempt on my part to carry water for bigots, or as an

1. On Sensitivity and Unity Regarding the Confederate Battle Flag, Resolution 7, Southern Baptist Convention, June 14, 2016. The full resolution is available here: http://erlc.com/resource-library/articles/resolution-7-on-sensitivity-and-unity-regarding-the-confederate-battle-flag.
2. James Bruce, "Confessions and Questions," World, July 23, 2016, https://world.wng.org/2016/07/confessions_and_questions.

attempt to justify what I know to be utterly contrary to the holiness of God, is . . . well, the kind of person who does that kind of thing. Watch for them in the comments.

My objection is not to any genuine repentance of any genuine sin whatever. My concern is that this kind of thing will simply represent a lot of thin-wash white bustle, an activity to which we are exceedingly prone, *and that it will lead to a perpetuation of the sins we pretend to decry.* "They have healed the wound of my people lightly, saying, 'Peace, peace,' when there is no peace" (Jer. 8:11, ESV).

I happen to believe that a good deal of racial repentance really is in order, but it sure won't be ushered in by any study committees on racial reconciliation who have been reading all the wrong sort of books. It will be brought in by a fundamentalist preacher, right out of a Flannery O'Connor short story, preaching hot gospel with his shirt sleeves rolled up and looking like nothing on earth. I don't care what color he is. What will matter is the color of his words.

AS DEFINED BY GOD

So I said that racism as defined by God is wickedness. Unfortunately, the word itself—because of the world's corruption of *all* words related to morality and moral choices—has become almost totally worthless.

Racism as defined by the world . . . actually, *there* is the problem. The world is unable to define racism. How could they? They have assiduously built a Great Tower out of the fog bricks of relativistic nonsense, but they still expect everyone to react with horror whenever they snap their fingers and declare that a moral outrage has been committed.

The only people this really works on anymore would be the evangelical moderates and SJWs.

Racism, as nebulously denounced by worldlings, isn't really anything at all. What is racism? Is it, as the wit had it, winning an argument with a liberal? Is it a failure to smell the white privilege wafting off Harvard Law School in the warmer months? Is it the Tea Party desire to get the budget to balance? You get my point—God hates racial vainglory and He hates racial malice. Everything else should just be considered a political cudgel that the left uses for keeping the unwashed peons in line.

SO WHAT IS THE REAL PROBLEM THEN?

My point is this. If we are going to repent of what caused the problem, then we need to repent of what actually caused the problem. When our society was openly racist— as it has been—the problem was that *it was all very popular*. It was Science. All the cool kids were in favor of it. When the world was all about something, there was always a wide swath within the church that desperately wanted to be all about the same thing for the sake of relevance.

Now if the original sin was capitulating to the world's pressure *then*, you don't really show repentance by capitulating to the world's pressure *now*. The problem then was the church's vulnerability to the cool shame. *That* is what must be addressed, and not primarily the content of the "shame."

When white people lurch from being patronizing and critical of blacks to being patronizing and laudatory, do we actually think that this somehow represents repentance? Perhaps the problem was that insufferable smell of complacent superiority that comes off both. Thinking that this change is repentance is like thinking that teenagers—who have begged their parents over the changing generations, in turns, to *pleeezzzze* let them have saddle shoes, bell bottoms, nose rings, and that neon purple spray paint operation for their hair—are somehow gaining wisdom. No, peer pressure just blows in different directions, and so those vulnerable to peer pressure blow over in different directions. Watching last year's compromises go out of fashion is not repentance, even if, like Esau, you look at your pet rock with tears in your eyes.

If you want to meet the kind of man who would have been out of step with prevailing nonsense then, you should look for the kind of man who is out of step with it *now*. People who are eager to be in step now are the same people who would have been eager to be in step then.

TOMBS OF THE PROPHETS

When Jesus taught us about the identity of the caretakers of the tombs of the prophets, what was he saying? What was His *argument*?

"Woe unto you, scribes and Pharisees, hypocrites! because ye build the tombs of the prophets, and garnish the sepulchres of the righteous, And say, If we had been in the days of our fathers, we would not have been partakers with them in the blood of the prophets. Wherefore ye be witnesses unto yourselves, that ye are the children of them which killed the prophets" (Matt. 23:29–31).

Jesus is not catching them out over a slight verbal misstep—"Aha! you said 'the days of *our fathers*'!" That wouldn't have demonstrated anything. *Jesus* was descended from men who persecuted the prophets (Matt. 1:10). Rather, He is saying that the garnishing of the tombs of the prophets was *driven by the very same thing* that caused their ancestors to stone the prophets in the first place. In one era, what the cool kids wanted was to kill those guys. In another era, what the cool kids wanted was to honor those guys, mostly for being dead now. Being dead made the prophets much more cooperative and likable. In both eras, they were accommodated by a certain kind of person characterized by an extraordinary degree of pliancy. There is a certain kind of person who will always Do What Is Expected.

You want him to recycle for the planet? He's there. You want him to dive into eugenics? He's with it. You want him to establish a man's character by counting the bumps on his head? Got it, check. You want him simply to accept what Approved Opinion has determined about (check all that apply) 1) the inferiority of blacks, 2) the rates of climate change, or 3) the undesirability of nuclear war. Approved Opinion never stays in one place, so you do have to be limber . . . but some people are ever-limber. They were born limbering up.

That is the foundational sin in all this that needs repentance—caring more about the world's opinion than you do about the Word's truth.

But there is a certain kind of man who knows how not to be stampeded. He is not valued greatly in any generation, for he consistently is a pain in the neck, but after he is dead and deep, the praise starts to trickle in.

ALT-RIGHTY THEN

In the summer of 2017, the SBC went on to denounce alt-right white supremacy, and did so overwhelmingly. As far as *that* goes, considered within a narrow compass, no problems. When alt-right racists get poked with any kind of stick, it is difficult for me to summon up any kind of sorrow.

> Racism and white supremacy are, sadly, not extinct but present all over the world in various white supremacist movements, sometimes known as "white nationalism" or "alt-right." The messengers to the Southern Baptist Convention . . .decry every form of racism, including alt-right white supremacy, as antithetical to the gospel of Jesus Christ . . . . We denounce and repudiate white supremacy and every form of racial and ethnic hatred as of the devil.[3]

But here is the problem. The SBC statement admirably denounces every form of racism in general, but specifically denounces only one kind of racism, the kind that has recently come bubbling to the surface in the alt-right movement. What this does is almost completely ignore where the alt-right movement is deriving its energy. So that pot is coming to a boil. What is the burner underneath that pot? How is it that they are attracting recruits? More about this in a moment.

Here is a thought experiment. Suppose someone introduced another resolution, next time around, identical in theology to this one, and identical in theological expression to this one, but with the only difference being that the specific groups denounced were the Nation of Islam or Black Lives Matter. The *same sin* is rejected, and for the

---

3. "On The Anti-gospel Of Alt-right White Supremacy," June 1, 2017, https://www.sbc.net/resource-library/resolutions/on-the-anti-gospel-of-alt-right-white-supremacy/

same reason—because of the denial of what the blood of Jesus Christ was intended to do. God intended to make one new man out of the two. Right?

Does anyone believe that such a resolution would sail through? I am afraid that it would not. There would be an uproar because, while the theology was righteous, there would be legitimate suspicion that there was a surreptitious (political) agenda in the selectivity of the identified villains. And so there would be.

And this is why, when representatives of Jesus Christ are denouncing hateful bigotries, and they take it upon themselves to repudiate what the star-bellied sneetches have done to the non-star-bellied sneetches, they must also take care to address any problems that have run the other way. *This must all be done at the same time.* Otherwise, the church is being *played.* In the New Testament, the Jews have to love and accept the Gentiles, and the Gentiles also have to love and accept the Jews. Everybody does this, and all at the same time. True communion at the Table of Christ must run in every direction. No one is permitted to come with any grievances in hand. All of us must set all of them down.

The leadership of the church must be seen as insisting on this. If we do not, what happens? Instead of presenting a gospel-oriented "third way," we are actually being used by various competing factions in the world. This is the cool shame at work again.

Evangelical Christians are adept at adopting worldly fashions ten years after the world has adopted them, and then doing it worse. This is true of fashion, music, diets, you name it. It is also true of political fads and fashions. As chronic late adapters, we are often climbing on board just as the carnal overreaction to the carnal stupidity is setting in. The world is about to throw off whatever it was as "dumb and stupid," while we are all clamoring to be included. "May we join you on board?" we ask the disembarking passengers.

For a generation or so, our society has been busy at *creating the preconditions* for the rise of the alt-right. We have done this by abandoning the early promises of the civil rights movement (to judge on the basis of content of character *only*), and by instituting a hard regime of political correctness, hating whitey, affirmative action, not to mention vitriolic denunciations of those "racists" who believe that budgets should balance.

So let me say it again. The alt-right is the bastard child of obsequious political correctness on race. *That* is where this is coming from. That is the root. That is where the energy is coming from. And so what are we doing in the church? Right when the explosive (and sinful) reaction has started to happen, we say (ten years late), that we need to copy what the world did in order to get us into this mess.

No. No thumb on the scales of racial reconciliation. Equal weights and measures. Evenhandedness. In Christ there is neither Jew nor Greek.

I already said that (considered in isolation) I found it hard to summon up any sorrow over denunciations of the alt-right. But I think it is only fair to add that I believe that one-sided denunciations of one sort of racial animosity is *not* something that will in any way dismay members of the alt-right. They will welcome it. That kind of thing is their food, their nourishment. And if you don't want weeds in your garden, then stop fertilizing and watering them.

SIMPER REFORMANDA

A reasonable rejoinder to my argument is that Southern Baptists, given their history, do not have the "distance" to deal with everyone in a "blind justice" even-handed manner. They are not the judge, trying to be impartial, but rather an ex-con still making restitution.[4]

This point does have some weight. The legacy of what we might call "old-school" racism is still within living memory. For the Southern Baptists to condemn the outrages of BLM might not look like evenhandedness, but rather like an old bad habit creeping back.

But the leadership of the Southern Baptists is required by God, in my view, to jealously guard equity in the process. This is because they are not in a quiet room, carefully settling accounts, placing weights on scales with history books spread out before them. They are engaged in the hurly burly of leading millions of people, some of whom remember the bad old days, and many of whom have no experience with racial issues other than the ones we are having now. In other words, when you start to wobble on a bicycle, overcorrecting in the other direction might be technically "just" (you might be yanking to the left only as far as you yanked to the right), but this is also the way you crash.

In Thomas Sowell's magisterial book *A Conflict of Visions*[5], he points out the radical difference between

---

4. This reasonable rejoinder was, in fact, made by Mike Leake on his blog, *Borrowed Light*: "Our Unbalanced Scales, or Why I Disagree with @douglaswils on the Alt-Right and #SBC17," June 21, 2017, http://www .mikeleake.net/2017/06/our-unbalanced-scales-or-why-i-disagree-with -douglaswils-on-the-alt-right-and-sbc17.html.
5. *A Conflict of Visions: Ideological Origins of Political Struggles* (Cambridge, MA: Basic Books, 2007).

those who want equality of outcome and those who want equality of process. The former hold to what he calls the unconstrained vision and the latter to the constrained vision. The former are trying to build a Utopia, and the latter are trying to avoid having Illinois become Venezuela. Those who follow the unconstrained vision are great at two things—great soaring rhetoric, and crashing bicycles.

My point is that a manifest lack of evenhandedness now is what enables extreme groups to recruit people you don't want them recruiting. The alt-right is attractive to many young people, and it is attractive for a reason. What is that reason? Decades of political correctness in our cultural and political leadership, that's what. Tim Bayly wonderfully tagged this phenomenon as *simper reformanda*.

YEAST WORKS SLOWLY

Another objection notes that my argument is "nice in idea in the abstract, but the power structure is still white-run and tilted in favor of whites generally (not toward any particular white individual, but toward the group), and therefore alt-right is *more* of an immediate problem than Nation of Islam or BLM."[6]

To this I would say that when power structures change naturally, slowly, and organically, there is still the potential for violence. When they are imposed with a heavy hand, the violent reaction is almost guaranteed. That is my argument about the rise of the alt-right. Where is this energy coming from? It is not coming from a faint memory of the old injustices—it is coming from a smarting experience

6. This is from private correspondence with a friend.

with the new injustices. It is not the job of political and religious leaders to be ambitious about their abilities to tinker with "power structures." When they undertake *that* kind of thing, they are getting in way over their heads. Their job is to be known as equitable, as men who will deal justly with the individuals who come in front of them, whatever the power structures might be doing.

Yeast works through the loaf slowly. When you pass laws about the appropriate yeast to dough ratios, you find yourself creating more troubles than you are solving.

THE DANGERS OF GROUP REPENTANCE

One last comment. C.S. Lewis once wrote a stupendous essay titled *Dangers of National Repentance*, which I would like to commend to all who think they might run the risk of falling into some intemperate passions after reading this post. The essay can be found in *God in the Dock*.

Lewis writes, "The first and fatal charm of national repentance is, therefore, the encouragement it gives us to turn from the bitter task of repenting our own sins to the congenial one of bewailing—but, first, of denouncing—the conduct of others."[7]

---

7. C.S. Lewis, "The Dangers of National Repentance" in *God in the Dock* (Grand Rapids: Eerdmans, 1970), 190.

CHAPTER 14

THE JESUS FRUIT
AND THE JESUS TREE

This essay was originally published on August 15, 2017, a few weeks after the Unite the Right rally in Charlottesville, Virginia.

The central problem with the white supremacists in Charlottesville is not so much that they hate blacks and Jews. Their *central* problem is that they hate God, and hate Jesus Christ. And the same thing goes for the anitfa agitators on the other side of the street. Scripture tells us what the emotional weather is always like outside of Jesus Christ: "For we ourselves also were sometimes foolish, disobedient, deceived, serving divers lusts and pleasures, *living in malice and envy, hateful, and hating one another*" (Titus 3:3).

There is no way out of this apart from real repentance. God sent His Son into this world, in part, in order to solve the most intractable of problems—that of ethnic animosity. Christ was sent in order to overcome the division between Jew and Gentile, to create one new man out of two (Eph. 2:15), and the chasm between *those* two groups was a true chasm. But—liberal bromides notwithstanding—we cannot have the Jesus fruit apart from the Jesus tree. "And the times of this ignorance God winked at; but now *commandeth all men every where to repent*" (Acts 17:30). "Neither is there salvation in any other: for there is *none other name* under heaven given among men, whereby we must be saved" (Acts 4:12). We are commanded to *repent*, and we are commanded to repent by *Jesus*. We cannot do anything resembling this if we persist in our refusal to name His name. We must come to hate our sin, which means *naming* it, and we must come to love Jesus, which means *naming* Him.

Refuse to do that and the only thing you have to look forward to is an ever-increasing cycle of hatreds, spilling out of hearts and into the streets. These racial animosities are not a sin against America, or democracy, or our social fabric. They are a sin against *God*.

So every form of race-hustling, independent of which race might be receiving the benefits of that hustle, is detestable to God. Every form of race-baiting is detestable to God. Every form of racial biting is detestable to God. And this includes, incidentally, the lite forms of race-hustling, race-baiting, and racial biting that have somehow become acceptable within the church. But Christless alt-right thinking defiles the sanctuary. Christless grievance politics defile the sanctuary. There are those who hustle outside the church, and there are those who shamble and shuffle inside it, playing the same game at a *slow* enough speed to be palatable to evangelicals. But do not ask how *fast* it is going. Ask rather what *direction* it is going. There are only two directions—the New Jerusalem or the Abyss.

Ask yourself, where did these white supremacists come from? Were they educated in white supremacist academies? Not a bit of it—I will lay you even money that they were educated under the government school program of identity politics, and they then went and looked in the mirror to find out what side they were on. And outside of Christ, that is the way it always has to go. Outside of Christ, attempts at racial reconciliation are always going to be a matter of reaching around Lady Justice in order to get your thumb on the *other* scale now. You keep saying you are going to fix everything, and you keep knocking everything over.

It might be said that I am saying these things as a white male in his sixties, and therefore my point is suspect and invalid. No, I am saying these things as a minister of Jesus Christ, and when He makes *His* appointments, it has nothing to do with racial quotas, and everything to do with the authority of His Word. And so here is a message from God—a hammer that breaks the rock of racial animosities into pieces (Jer. 23:29). And it is the *only* hammer that can break this rock.

So here is the message for those who hate image bearers of God because they don't like the color God used to paint that particular image. So then, you have taken it upon yourself to hate God in this way? Very well. Have it your way. Scripture teaches that—for those insist upon living in their own little cesspool of animosity—God hates them also.

Someone might object that they have been taught that God loves sinners, including those who sin racially, unconditionally. No, God loves sinners *in Christ*. God so loved the world that *He gave His only begotten Son*. The only place where a sinner can possibly be a recipient of God's love is in Christ. God's love for sinners was bestowed and manifested in one place only, and that place was the cross of Christ. And so what happens to those who hate Christ, who despise His cross, who insist on turning their face away from Him? What happens to those who stand aloof from God's *solitary provision* for sinners? They remain outside in the twilight—a twilight that is rapidly becoming the outer darkness. Where they stand, they hate God, and God hates them.

You heard that right. God hates evil men. "The Lord trieth the righteous: But the wicked *and him that loveth violence his soul hateth*" (Ps. 11:5). Those who love violence do so for various reasons, and they have all their rationalizations in place. But they rationalize under the wrath of God. They are by nature objects of wrath (Rom. 9:22). The white man who loves violence is detested by God. The black man who loves violence is detested by God. The fact that they detest each other does not keep them from going to Hell together.

Tim Challies sums it up nicely: God "hates wicked people from his soul, from the very depth of his being. God hates their ways (Proverbs 15:9), their thoughts (Proverbs 15:26), their worship (Proverbs 15:8), their actions (Proverbs 6:18), and their evil deeds (Psalm 5:5)."[1]

---

1. Tim Challies, "God Hates Wicked People," *Challies* (blog), February 11, 2017, https://www.challies.com/articles/god-hates-wicked-people.

There is only one righteous side for Christians to take in a situation like this, and that is the side of the gospel of reconciliation. The only way that racial animosity can ever die is if it is nailed to the cross where Jesus died. And again, for that to happen, the sin must have a name and the Savior must have a name.

Anything else is trying to pick up the turd by the clean end.

APPENDIX

THE DESIRING GOD
POSTS

n September 2013, I spoke at Desiring God's annual
national conference. In the context of that event, I had
the privilege of meeting together with a number of men
to discuss various issues surrounding the central topic of
racial reconciliation. The most immediate reason for the
meeting was an online interaction I had recently had with
Thabiti Anyabwile[1], coupled with reactions to the fact that
I had been invited to speak at Desiring God. Because the
ministries associated with the leadership of John Piper
have long been known for their zeal in pursuing the
hard work of racial harmony, it should not be surprising
that there were a range of feelings about my coming to
Minneapolis—from opposed, to concerned, to ambivalent,

1. A summary of this exchange and links to the individual posts can
be found at https://www.thegospelcoalition.org/blogs/thabiti-anyabwile
/a-black-and-tan-round-up.

135

to supportive. And in some quarters, there was consternation, some of it pretty intense.

In response to all this, a meeting was arranged with about a dozen of us in order to hash things out. I am very grateful to those who organized the meeting and to those who were willing to attend it. In that attendance were black pastors and seminarians. There were also whites engaged in urban work who were distressed at how my stance makes their work more difficult. There were some of the men involved with inviting me to Minneapolis in the first place.

Following that meeting, I wrote a series of four blog posts, which have been combined and edited into this appendix. Many of the topics already covered in the book are also addressed here, but the series seemed to warrant a separate presentation.

A FRUITFUL START

I begin with two aspects of our conversation.

The first is a reiteration of something I told Thabiti in our exchanges. When I write polemically against the PC-left, as I often do, I do it with mayhem in mind, and have no desire to take back a syllable of it. But if I find that my words have also given offense in quarters where I had and have *no* desire to give offense, I want to be eager to seek pardon or forgiveness, as appropriate. I hope that was clear in our meeting on Friday, and in a conviction that a second coat of good paint never hurts, I want to make it clear again now. It is no part of my purpose to create unnecessary barriers to fellowship for men like Thabiti—and I was privileged to meet with some men like him last Friday.

The second thing has to do with the value of meeting face to face. This is something the Scriptures clearly point us to as we engage in delicate operations like this. Paul wanted to be present with the Galatians, so he could change his tone with them (Gal. 4:20). John longed to be with his friends (2 John 12), but in the meantime a letter would have to do. The apostle Paul earnestly wanted to be present with the Thessalonians (1 Thess. 2:17). Good communication *can* occur via the written word, but for some things, talking in person is always better. It certainly was in this instance and, I think, in any other situation like it.

Written denunciations of racism can come off as perfunctory and obligatory, like a white man dutifully ticking boxes. That's how some have heard me. But in person, if you really hate racial vainglory (as I really *do*), then it becomes possible to communicate more effectively.

Also, stating that we had a profitable meeting should not be taken as an indication that we reached agreement on everything or that the need for such meetings is over. I am simply saying that when we arrived together, there was a lot more tension than when we left. We left in fellowship with one another, which is a God-ordained stepping stone toward likemindedness. And I think the Spirit was pleased with that.

ZERO-SUM COMPASSION

Lord willing, this will be the second of four posts. In the last of them I want to restate and expand an apology that I offered to Thabiti in the course of our exchanges. Because I would like that apology to do as much good and make as much sense as it possibly can, I want to set the stage for it first. Please bear with me.

With this post, I want to begin with my conclusion, and then work backward toward the problem. If we want to undertake the perilous task of working toward racial and ethnic harmony, I want to submit that we must do it by means of a radical God-centeredness. So I want to begin there and then work back to some of the stumbling blocks that keep us from appealing to such a God-centeredness. As a consequence, these stumbling blocks also prevent us from actually getting anywhere. Our labors at racial harmony are often like that woman in the gospels—the more the physicians treated her, the worse it got.

This world has been a world full of tears. The histories that could be written of outrage, oppression, treachery, cruelty, hatred, malice, torture, genocide, slavery, and rape are histories that could fill many volumes. Not only so, but I don't believe that any one of us is capable of reading them all with any kind of true comprehension, and a true attempt would crush us.

But the grace of God is much greater than the sin of man. Scripture promises that in Christ every last one of these wrongs will be put right. Only in Christ will this happen, but in Christ it will happen completely. The promise is this: God Himself will dry every tear. He has stored up all the tears of all His saints in a bottle (Ps. 56:8), and He has never lost track of any. He catalogs them all. We lose track almost right away, but He never does.

He will not just dry the most recent tear we shed, or the tears we happened to be shedding when the world ended, but rather He will right every wrong, dry every tear, set every bone, and heal every wound. Nothing will be left out or left over. We are called to believe this by faith—and I believe that if we do, it will shape every work in a cruciform mold.

> And one of the elders answered, saying unto me, What are these which are arrayed in white robes? and whence came they? And I said unto him, Sir, thou knowest. And he said to me, These are they which came out of great tribulation, and have washed their robes, and made them white in the blood of the Lamb. Therefore are they before the throne of God, and serve him day and night in his temple: and he that sitteth on the throne shall dwell among them. They shall hunger no more, neither thirst any more; neither shall the sun light on them, nor any heat. For the Lamb which is in the midst of the throne shall feed them, and shall lead them unto living fountains of waters: *and God shall wipe away all tears from their eyes.* (Rev. 7:13–17)

> And I heard a great voice out of heaven saying, Behold, the tabernacle of God is with men, and he will dwell with them, and they shall be his people, and God himself shall be with them, and be their God. *And God shall wipe away all tears from their eyes*; and there shall be no more death, neither sorrow, *nor crying*, neither shall there be any more pain: for the former things are passed away. (Rev. 21:3–4)

This destination is where human history is going, and in the midst of our tears, this can be difficult for us to see.

But what we cannot do, God in fact can do. And what God can in fact do, He has promised to do in His Son, our Lord Jesus. Now, how might we tell when we are starting to forget this? This is an important question because we stumble at this point quite a lot.

Our emotions, just like the rest of us, are finite. They have limits. The horrible things that go on in the world in the course of just one evening, in just one big city, are enough to cause us outrage overload. The weight of this world's horrors cannot be carried by us. I believe this is the case even if we were not thinking of individual instances, but rather of just the categories—rapes, molestations, murders, and so on.

We cannot carry everything, but God still insists that we carry *something*. We are to weep with those who weep (Rom. 12:15). God wants us to be a neighbor to those who suffer without aspiring to the position of a god in the lives of those who suffer. And in the parable of the Good Samaritan, Jesus defines *neighbor* as the one in front of us right now.

In order to explain how this works, I first have to explain the idea of a zero-sum game. This phrase means that when a particular resource is limited, it occurs to everyone (sooner rather than later) that more for him means less for me. If the size of the pie is fixed, then if he gets a bigger piece of it, then somebody else will have to take a smaller piece. This concept is usually appealed to when we are talking about wealth and economics, and in my attacks on envy I have often discussed it elsewhere under that heading. But it applies to things like human compassion also.

When particular horrors occur, God calls His saints to minister in the midst of the suffering. It might be a natural disaster, like a tornado taking out a town, or the result of human evil, as when somebody shoots up an elementary school.

Only one part of the Body of Christ is there, but all of God is there. The omnipresence of God is not like pie dough—the farther you spread it, the thinner it is. No, the doctrine of God's omnipresence means that all of God is in every place. But He particularly manifests His presence through the hands, feet, and voices of His people, placed there to minister in His name.

Now all of God can be with us, but all of us cannot be with God in every other place. We can tell that we have started to slip when we start to think we can, and when we start to blame others for not being where we are. Here is the telltale sign. We are starting to slide when we start to judge our brother's motives by whether or not he experiences the same gut response of reactive compassion to the outrage we are assigned to deal with. But a Christian nurse in Romania who has dedicated herself to caring for abandoned orphans with birth defects may never have heard of *Roe v. Wade*. She doesn't need to.

We tend to think there is only so much compassion to go around, and more of it over there (expended on the abortion cause) must mean less of it over here (with our cause). The fact that we can fall into this does not mean that our cause (whatever it is) is illegitimate. But it does mean that I can give all my money to the poor, and wind up with nothing in my heavenly account, anyway (1 Cor. 13:3).

Imagine two Christians, both fighting the kind of heartache that God hates. One is fighting poverty in the inner city and the other is fighting an abortion clinic in a wealthier part of the state. There is the obvious problem of physical resources, which every ministry fundraiser has had to deal with—any number of legitimate and God-honoring ministries are seeking support from the same givers, from the same donors. And it is easy to think that more for "them" means less for "us."

But I am speaking here of the emotional resources. There are Jews who hate it when the abortion carnage is called a holocaust. There is only one holocaust, and their great grandmother died in it. In the conversation with John Piper the other night, I said that abortion is "our middle passage." This could be heard (but was not intended to be heard) as minimizing the horrors of the historical middle passage of the slave trade. When I talk this way, someone could hear me saying that there could be two—but when a horror is unique, there cannot be two. How could there be two?

Moreover, by trying to get Christians to fully engage emotionally with the abortion bloodbath, because our emotional resources are limited I might be seen as taking away or "minimizing" the other horrors that other Christians (really) are called to address. Let's say the Gosnell outrage caused greater focus on how the ghouls prey on black children in urban areas. When this happens, we should simply thank the Lord, recognizing that this is a good thing. We can do this, even though some attention might be taken away from other good causes, and even though some of the people organizing this newest effort might be classed as "operators." I think it was Eric Hoffer who said something like "first a movement, then a business, then a racket."

This has happened in pro-life circles, and it has happened in the arena of race relations. It complicates the work of racial harmony enormously. It always complicates everything. As I look out at the racial landscape, I do see wise pastors like Thabiti. But I also see the Sharptons and the Jacksons—the race-baiters and hustlers. Then in the middle, I see sincere believers who are more affected by the hustlers than perhaps they ought to be. How is it possible to speak as to be clearly understood by all? As far as the hustlers go, it is not possible. How can you persuade a man whose livelihood depends upon him remaining unpersuaded?

I believe that we are in this difficult place because we have not submitted to the God-centeredness I mentioned. If I am intoxicated by His glory, then I will not fume if I meet a black man who has not experienced the indignities that his grandfather suffered daily, and his father experienced regularly—I will take it as real progress, and not a sign that he is a Tom. If we are submissive to the great promises of God, then we will not resent those who hate injustice, even if they hate it and fight it in a different place in the line.

I have argued that American history is a long and complicated three-dimensional chess game, and we are being forced into appalling choices today because we weren't thinking clearly fifteen moves ago. Many of us are not thinking clearly now. This may not make sense when someone first hears me trying to explain this, *but please hear me out.* How is it possible for the vast majority of African American Christians to have supported President Obama the *second* time, the most radically pro-abortion president we could possibly have, and to do this when the disproportionate number of his victims are black infants facing their own middle passage *alone*? How were they maneuvered into this complicity? For it *is* complicity, and it requires repentance. The God who catalogs the tears is not overlooking the tears of these His little ones.

And this is why this extended argument is necessary. When I say that this outrage now is something we must turn away from in repentant disgust, I am in no way trying to minimize the outrages that our great-grandfathers should have turned away from. And if we think our great grandfathers should not have had such a hard time repenting, then maybe we should demonstrate for everybody how simple and easy it is.

I am finite and cannot fight evil everywhere. But I can reject it everywhere and be preparing my heart to shout the *amen* when the Almighty God tears the sky open and comes down to put everything to rights. He *will* do so, and as this world groans, longing for the Lord's coming, we who have the first fruits of the Spirit groan, also.

Wickedness committed in the past is never a license for us to give way to wickedness now. In Canto 33 of the *Inferno*, Dante tells a chilling story about a damned soul named Ugolino. He is in the lowest pit of Hell, where he is spending eternity gnawing on the brain of the man who murdered him. That man was Archbishop Ruggieri, and he killed Ugolino and his young sons by starving them all to death in a tower. As Dante tells the story, your heart really goes out to Ugolino and his sons. The way they died was a true horror. And then the story ends . . . with Ugolino in Hell, locked up in the tower of his own bitterness forever and ever. Dante is a master poet in how he tells us this story. When Ugolino wakes up in the prison, he hears his sons sobbing in their sleep, asking for bread. Then when he hears the door of the tower being nailed shut, he says, "I did not weep, I turned to stone inside." But what father, when his son asks him for bread, will give him a stone instead (Luke 11:11)?

What then is our duty in this? It is to say *amen* beforehand to what God is going to do, when He deals with all of it, and we do this by behaving with a heart of true compassion toward our neighbor. And we cannot play dumb, wondering who our neighbor is—that will become vividly clear the moment the clarion trumpet goes.

There is only one place in the New Testament where God's people cry out, "Alleluia!" That place is where the people of God are looking at the smoke of the Great Babylon, rising up forever. "And again they said, Alleluia. And her smoke rose up for ever and ever" (Rev. 19:3). One of the things that this Babylon was noted for was her great ability in merchandising the souls of men (Rev. 18:13).

Every slave ship. Every abortion clinic. Every ankle chain. Every saline injection. Every kidnapping. Every ethnic cleansing. Every concentration camp. Every kangaroo court. Every church burning. Every rape room. Every dungeon pit. Every tear.

The smoke from her goes up forever and ever. *Alleluia.*

LEAVEN IN THE FLOUR

This is the third of four pieces on the subject of American slavery and modern race relations. I am building up to my conclusion, in which I will restate and expand a variation of an apology I extended to Thabiti in the course of our exchanges. But why all this preparation beforehand? Well, if I seek forgiveness for x, and if anybody hears me seeking forgiveness for x,y, and z, then I will be in real trouble (just a few weeks later) if I re-offend by reasserting y and z all over again. So consider this post and my previous post as a restatement of y and z at the front end.

What follows is, in summary form, a statement about what I actually believe with regard to the teaching of the New Testament about slavery. I want to do this as though this were the first time I had ever said anything about it. I do not regard this as a personal quirk of my own, but rather as the teaching of Scripture which is binding on us all—red and yellow, black and white. This is what I believe careful exegesis requires.

The sufficiency of Scripture is an abstract doctrine if we never ground what we are saying *in the text*. So in my mind, the heart of this entire debate concerns the sufficiency of Scripture. Sufficiency is a doctrine that is easy to proclaim until it gets you in trouble, and it usually causes the trouble when you get to the point of contested applications.

Now Scripture can be sufficient for every contingency only if it is the very breath of God. But if we believe that it is inspired in that way, then we should be determined as Christians to live and die by it. When we are in situations that appear to us to be absolutely intractable, whether individual or cultural, then we must turn to the Bible for instruction in how we should respond. How should we then live?

There are many directions this discussion could take, and I don't mind taking them each at the appropriate time. But there is only one thing that matters as a root issue. What we say when we have addressed this one issue will actually determine whether further discussion will be profitable.

This root issue does not require us to compare the historical day-to-day conditions of Roman and American slaves. I happen to believe that American slavery (as it was legally structured) was worse in certain key respects, and that Roman slavery (as it was legally structured) was worse in others. For an instance of the former, take the horrific conditions suffered by the slaves in the middle passage. Take the absolute authority of the paterfamilias for an example of the latter—American slaveowners were legally constrained in ways that the Romans were not. But such detailed comparisons are actually not necessary to my argument—such a comparison would only be relevant if either system required the abuse of slaves as mandatory.

Because abuse was not mandatory (either in Rome or in America), it was therefore possible for a Christian owner of slaves to heed the ameliorating teaching given by the apostle Paul. In both systems, slave owners had the liberty to treat their slaves well. This would obviously include treating them well in the way their church leaders required. Obedience in the midst of a corrupt and fallen system was therefore possible in A.D. 50 and in A.D. 1850.

If it were not possible, the apostles would have not told anyone to do it. This means that it was possible for a man in South Carolina to treat his slave in exactly the same way that Paul required Philemon to treat Onesimus. And the guy who was willing to do that is the only guy I am willing to defend and stand with.

Moreover, there is no reason for taking such obedience in the midst of such circumstances as requiring an approval of all the surrounding disobedience. To say that obedience was righteous is not to say that disobedience was also righteous.

So the apostles were faced with a circumstance where slaves and slaveowners were members of their churches.

When confronted with this, what did they tell everybody to do? How did they handle it? This was a common enough problem that *it was explicitly addressed in at least seven books of the New Testament.* Here it is in brief:

> Were you a bondservant [*doulos*] when called? Do not be concerned about it. (But if you can gain your freedom, avail yourself of the opportunity.) For he who was called in the Lord as a bondservant [*doulos*] is a freedman of the Lord. Likewise he who was free when called is a bondservant of Christ. You were bought with a price; do not become bondservants [*doulos*] of men. So, brothers, in whatever condition each was called, there let him remain with God. (1 Cor. 7:21–24)

> Bondservants [*doulos*], obey your earthly masters [*kurios*] with fear and trembling, with a sincere heart, as you would Christ, not by the way of eye-service, as people-pleasers . . . . (Eph. 6:5–6a, ESV)

> Masters [*kurios*], do the same to them, and stop your threatening, knowing that he who is both their Master and yours is in heaven, and that there is no partiality with him. (Eph. 6:9, ESV)

> Bondservants [*doulos*], obey in everything those who are your earthly masters [*kurios*], not by way of eye-service, as people-pleasers, but with sincerity of heart, fearing the Lord. (Col. 3:22, ESV)

> Masters [*kurios*], treat your bondservants [*doulos*] just-

ly and fairly, knowing that you also have a Master in heaven. (Col. 4:1, ESV)

Let all who are under a yoke as bondservants [*doulos*] regard their own masters [*despotes*] as worthy of all honor, so that the name of God and the teaching may not be reviled. Those who have believing masters [*despotes*] must not be disrespectful on the ground that they are brothers; rather they must serve all the better since those who benefit by their good service are believers and beloved. (1 Tim. 6:1-2, ESV)

Bondservants [*doulos*] are to be submissive to their own masters [*despotes*] in everything; they are to be well-pleasing, not argumentative, not pilfering, but showing all good faith, so that in everything they may adorn the doctrine of God our Savior. (Titus 2:9–10)

For this perhaps is why he was parted from you for a while, that you might have him back forever, no longer as a bondservant [*doulos*] but more than a bondservant [*doulos*], as a beloved brother—especially to me, but how much more to you, both in the flesh and in the Lord. (Philem. 15–16)

Servants [*oiketes*], be subject to your masters with all respect, not only to the good and gentle but also to the unjust. (1 Pet. 2:18, ESV)

Now there are three basic ways for believers to respond to such passages. One is to come up with some version of "That was then, this is now." This is to abandon the

sufficiency of Scripture, and it will not be long before biblical standards are being jettisoned in other areas, as well.
I say this only because you can see that kind of thing happening pretty much everywhere you look.

The second way is how too many Southern defenders of
slavery took it—arguing that slavery was designed by God
to be a permanent fixture in human affairs, thus keeping
everything just the way it was (with no thought of gradualism). They took some stills from the movie, and analyzed
them closely, but never watched the movie itself.

The third way would be to argue that this apostolic
strategy was actually a subversive attack on the institution
of slavery, an attack by means of gospel gradualism. All we
ask, the early Christians said, is to be allowed to put this
leaven here into the three measures of flour.

If you were to go for this third option, *then I would
agree completely*, and would say that this is precisely how
I have been seeking to apply these passages throughout
this entire controversy. I believe that it does justice to the
plain sense of the words, while at the same time display-
ing real trust in the power and trajectory of the gospel to
transform every human institution, including the really
problematic ones.

But, I would point out mildly, to argue for peacefully
subverting an institution until it is stone cold dead and good
riddance is not the same thing as defending that institution.

In short, when it comes to slavery in America, there is
no species of cruelty, unkindness, malice, hard-hearted-
ness, callousness, greed, avarice, presumption, lust, wickedness, arrogance, or pride that I am prepared to defend or

THE DESIRING GOD POSTS

explain away. The only thing that can deal with such sins is the blood of Jesus Christ.

But I know that I can be accused of complicity with such sins in history because of the *gradualism* in my gospel gradualism. To the extent that I have succeeded in echoing the teaching of the apostles on this point, I am willing to be misunderstood and misrepresented along with them. I believe that the Bible is God's Word, and I believe it is sufficient to undo every snarl.

But to the extent that I have given any *unnecessary* offense to brothers who were not caught up in the errors I have been addressing—because I have explained these truths in a way that would have made the apostle Paul cringe—I want to be easily entreated, as James put it, and I want to be eager to put things right. Because apologies are rarely improved when they are encumbered with accompanying "explanations," I have now said what I needed to say beforehand.

SINCERE PUBLIC APOLOGIES

This is the final post in a series of four on race and reconciliation. Sincere public apologies in matters like this are difficult for many reasons, some of which I discussed in my exchanges with Thabiti. We live in a time when many are hyper about race, and so whenever you address the topic publicly, you are speaking to a public which includes the PC-police, race-hustlers, white-guiltists, sheer opportunists, men of good will who have been affected more than they ought to have been by the hustlers, and men of sound sense and good will. The challenge is to speak to the last group, *genuinely*, without giving an inch to the first four groups, and in such a way as to create opportunities for fruitful reconciliation with the penultimate group. As we should all know by now, demanding apologies is one of the central techniques of modern polemical warfare, and the man who simply capitulates because the hounds have started baying is both a coward and a fool.

Nevertheless, in those places or areas where apologies are owed in the sight of God, they are owed regardless of what the unscrupulous might do with them. Whenever there are men of genuine good will, men engaged in the difficult task of genuine racial reconciliation, men who are willing to both hear and say hard things, who are willing to stay at the table despite the tension, who work hard to understand and express other people's views with accuracy and fairness, and who are willing to pray together and embrace as brothers when such a difficult meeting is over, the situation is quite different. To such men, men like Thabiti and brothers I met with in Minneapolis, I want you to know that I deeply regret my failures to anticipate your legitimate concerns, natural feelings, and understandable perspective on some of the things that I have written. I regret the barriers that were erected between us as a consequence, and I hope that this apology can go some of the way toward removing those barriers and setting us on a course to greater fellowship in the gospel of Jesus Christ.

That is a general statement, so I need to make it more specific. When I first started speaking and writing on this topic, the group of people I was reaching was very small and pretty insulated. There was no Internet, there was no blogging, and I had written only a few books, the reach of which was either limited or uncertain. If we did a

THE DESIRING GOD POSTS

conference on American history (which we would do), we were pleased to have fifty people in attendance. In short, we were nowhere near any kind of national microphones. We were backwater historians, back porch theologians.

Despite this, I saw clearly (with an eye of faith) that what we were doing and saying would at some point have a significant impact . . . with the first groups I listed above. I was a nobody, but I had every expectation that the PC-police would know my name at some future date, and I was deliberately preparing some stinkers for them. This was not being done for the sake of cheap entertainment—I have mentioned in other settings the kind of thing we were dealing with in our "insulated" circles (e.g., Paul Hill). So there were reasons for it, and I am not sorry about that in the least.

But this being the case, I ought to have guarded against being simultaneously farsighted and myopic. If I could anticipate some things that were still decades in the future (as I did), then I had an obligation to anticipate other aspects of my future as well. If I could see the one, then I had a responsibility to see the other. That is where my basic failure was, and that is what the apology is for.

I did guard myself against accusations of racism (in multiple ways), but there is a difference between anticipatory *defenses* against the PC-police and the hustlers, and anticipatory *love* toward those who have been directly affected by real racism, and who are my brothers in Christ. And to whatever extent I have been responsible for any barriers there, I am happy to do my part to take them down.